Bidean nam Bian, Glencoe.

SCOTTISH MOUNTAINEERING CLUB

DISTRICT GUIDE BOOKS

THE
Central Highlands

by Campbell R. Steven

THE SCOTTISH MOUNTAINEERING TRUST

EDINBURGH

First published in Great Britain in 1968 by
THE SCOTTISH MOUNTAINEERING TRUST

Copyright © 1968 by The Scottish Mountaineering Trust

First Edition   1934
Second Edition   1952
Third Edition   1968
Revised   1972

Designed for the Scottish Mountaineering Trust by
West Col Productions

WHOLESALE DISTRIBUTORS
West Col Productions
1 Meadow Close
Goring on Thames
Reading Berks England
RG8 OAP

Set in Monotype Plantin Series 110 and Grotesque 215
and printed Offset Litho in England by
Cox & Wyman Ltd, London, Fakenham and Reading

FOREWORD

WHEN THE PREVIOUS EDITIONS of the Central Highlands Guide were issued in 1934 and 1952, edited by Harry MacRobert, the world of mountains was a very different one to that which we find today. For one thing the amount of factual information on the Central Highlands is now too large to fit into one volume. Thus for certain areas like Glencoe and Ben Nevis the climbs have been extracted and made into books in their own right. For another, the growth of tourism and free time has filled what in times past were empty camp-sites and silent precipices. There are now so many tastes to be catered for. And thirdly, the land upon which these mountains stand, save in one instance, is now so little the property of and so outwith the control of the people of Scotland, that climbers are in danger of being beggars in their own land. Nevertheless the high tops are there for all to enjoy, and this totally revised volume is presented by the Guide Book Committee of the Scottish Mountaineering Club in the hope that every sort of person interested in the hills of this region will find a useful and definitive account of them.

The committee were lucky to be able to persuade so knowledgeable a person as Campbell Steven, a writer and long time member of the SMC to carry out the task. The book was entirely rewritten in the spring and summer of 1968, and if the General Editor has any apology to make, it is to Mr. Steven for pushing him faster than he felt it wise to go.

Glasgow, September 1968.

CONTENTS

ILLUSTRATIONS

LINE DIAGRAMS

INTRODUCTION

Area

The country included in this Guide to the Central Highlands lies mainly in Inverness-shire and Argyll, with a small eastern corner over the Perthshire border. The actual boundaries are as follows:

South – from Bridge of Orchy down Glen Orchy to Dalmally and thence along the line of the Oban railway to Connel;
West – Loch Linnhe and the Great Glen;
North – from Whitebridge, on Loch Ness-side, to Aviemore round the northern edge of the Monadh Liath;
East – the A9 Inverness–Perth road from Aviemore down to Dalnacardoch, thence to Kinloch Rannoch, west to Rannoch Station and so by the line of the West Highland railway back to Bridge of Orchy.

The Mountains

The Guide Book embraces Sections 4, 5 and 6 of Munro's Tables, covering 71 separate mountains – denoted by asterisks in the lists heading each chapter – and a further 71 subsidiary tops. In addition there are in the area 34 separate mountains of over 2500 feet, in accordance with the list compiled by the late J. Rooke Corbett. These are also included in the chapter headings and given brief mention in the text – not by any means an ideal arrangement, but better perhaps than a purely arbitrary selection on the grounds of interest or personal preference.

Hill-Walking

For endless variety in hill-walking and in rock, snow and ice climbing of every standard of difficulty, the area is unrivalled anywhere in Britain.

No matter the season of the year the hill-walker will find everything he could wish for – individual mountains of character such as Buachaille Etive Mòr or Stob Ghabhar or Ben Alder; superb viewpoints such as Beinn a' Bheithir or Ben Nevis itself; the choice of innumerable rewarding ridge-walks, on Ben Cruachan maybe, or the Mamores, or the Grey Corries; the spaciousness and wide horizons offered by the sweeping moorland heights of the Monadh Liath.

But the interest of the district goes far beyond the mere collection of tops and ridges, even beyond acquaintance with the more obvious attractions like Glencoe. For those who choose the remote places of the Highlands the discoveries to be made are endless: Loch Etive, for example, is still roadless – so is the heart of Rannoch Moor; cross the Devil's Staircase alone and keep company with the drovers and the soldiers and the Kinlochleven navvies who knew it long ago; follow in the Wordsworths' footsteps over the old road from Kingshouse to Forest Lodge, cutting across the immense, lonely semi-circle of Coire Bà; or choose – and enjoy – one of the great cross-country treks like the Corrieyairack, or Fort William–Corrour, or Corrour–Dalwhinnie by the Bealach Dubh. And if a little added piquancy is still looked for, there are always such variants as the harvest moon or keen February frost.

Rock, Snow and Ice Climbing

So far as the details of rock, snow and ice routes are concerned, the policy adopted in the Guide Book has been to describe in brief general terms only those areas already covered by the special climbing guides: Glencoe (including Beinn Trilleachan), Ben Nevis, Creag Meaghaidh and Creag Dubh. The route selections which have been made are intended to provide as wide a variety as possible to suit all capabilities and also to show something of the pattern of history. It is hoped that most of the classic climbs, still so well worth doing, have been given appropriate mention.

On the other hand, the attempt has been made to include in more satisfying detail descriptions of all other areas not covered by the rock-guides – an attempt that is all too liable to error and omission in these days of almost incredible proliferation of new low-level routes.

Grading has been kept as simple as possible; 'left' and 'right' refer to the climber facing upwards.

Snow and ice climbing of every degree of difficulty is, of course, to be found in the area. For the tyro there are many easy gullies from which to graduate, in due time, to more serious routes such as the Upper Couloir of Stob Ghabhar or Crowberry Gully, then – but only then – to the more severe problems of Glencoe, Ben Nevis and Creag Meaghaidh. This need to learn by gradual experience is a point which, unfortunately, cannot be stressed too often: all too many aspiring mountaineers – skilled possibly on the hardest of Welsh or Lakeland rock routes – keep finding to their cost that the winter severities of Scotland have a more lethal hostility than ever was imagined.

Ski-ing

For the downhill-only skier there is, on Meall a' Bhùiridh, some of the best piste running that Scotland has to offer. The north-facing slopes, compact and easily accessible, hold the snow well, and mechanization has gone far towards ensuring their popularity.

Elsewhere in the Central Highlands area there is almost unlimited scope for ski-exploration. Innumerable expeditions, short and long, have already been found eminently worth-while; many more wait to be tried. From Meall a' Bhùiridh to Stob Ghabhar; from Corrour to Tulloch over Stob Coire Sgriodain; across Ben Alder; on Aonach Mòr – while it remains unmechanized; on the Monadh Liath moors. It is only, perhaps, a question of time before some of the list is given a place in the *Haute Route Ecossaise* recently mooted but still no more than a particularly pleasant possibility.

Geology *by Campbell Forrest, B.Sc.*

Broadly, the Central Highlands are composed of three main groups of rock types: Moine and Dalradian schists, gneisses, and quartzites; granite of Old Red Sandstone Age; and lavas and volcanic ashes, also of Old Red Sandstone Age. These different rock types have influenced the character of the mountains which they build.

The schists and gneisses, which occupy much of the northern and eastern parts of the area, weather relatively easily to give a uniform soil, and the mountains are generally grassy and rounded. The Monadh Liath and Ben Alder groups are typical of hills composed of these rocks, whereas the great cliffs of Creag Meaghaidh are exceptional. Crags which appear attractive from a distance are generally too broken and vegetatious for summer climbing, almost the only exception being Creag Dubh near Newtonmore, although they may give fine winter climbing. On Binnein Shuas, near Loch Laggan, the crags are composed mainly of a remarkable pegmatite vein complex, and many of the holds on the climbs are huge single feldspar crystals. The Grey Corries and Mamore groups are formed largely of quartzite, more resistant than the schists and gneisses, resulting is sharp ridges flanked by bare scree slopes.

Granite of Old Red Sandstone Age outcrops in an almost continuous belt north-eastwards from Ben Cruachan to the Glen Roy area. In Glen Etive the granite is composed of two main units. The younger unit, the coarse Starav Granite, is ringed by the older unit, the Cruachan Granite, which extends from Ben Cruachan to Clach Leathad. The granite forms characteristically slabby hillsides, and it is the Starav Granite which forms the vast overlapping sheets on the south-east face of Beinn Trilleachan. The Moor of Rannoch granodiorite is earlier than the Etive complex and contrasts with it, being almost entirely below 2000 feet, and forming, for the main part, a basin. It occupies most of the Moor from the Black Mount north to Loch Ossian and north-east to Loch Rannoch and Loch Ericht, and extends a finger north-westwards towards Loch Laggan.

Glencoe is built of lavas and volcanic ashes of Old Red Sandstone Age, and is a classic example of the phenomenon of cauldron-subsidence. The elliptical outcrop is ringed by a fracture within which the cylindrical block of lavas sank into a magma chamber. The magma displaced by the subsidiary block rose along the fracture and forms an irregular ring of porphyrite which crosses the glen half a mile east of Altnafeadh and also just west of Loch Achtriochtan, where the fault itself forms the Chasm of An t-Sròn. Almost all the rock-climbing in Glencoe is on rhyolite, an acidic lava which is slow to weather and discourages vegetation, and so gives clean cliffs. The rhyolite is interbedded with considerable thicknesses of andesite, a more basic lava, which forms a few cliffs including the Church Door Buttress and the crags of Stob Coire nan Lochan, but generally forms steep vegetated slopes such as the lower parts of the North and West Faces of Aonach Dubh. Ben Nevis also shows a cauldron-subsidence structure, with the lavas which form the cliffs surrounded by an inner and a broken outer ring of granite.

To the north the Central Highlands are bounded by the Great

Glen Fault, and associated with this are the parallel Lochan na h-Earba and Ericht-Laidon Faults. The belts of shattered rock along these faults have been excavated by the ice and deepened into troughs, often loch-filled. Part of Glen Etive has been gouged out along the continuation of the Lochan na h-Earba Fault, and the Ericht-Laidon Fault continues south-west along Glen Strae. During the Ice Age the Rannoch Moor basin was filled with ice from the surrounding mountains. Glaciers moved radially from the centre, deepening and straightening the valleys and scouring the land surface.

Maps

Six-inch O.S. Although many Scottish sheets still belong to the old 'County' edition dating from the beginning of the century, the country is now being widely covered by post-Second World War sheets based on the National Grid. All of these, except some of the coastal sheets, are square, with sides representing 5 kilometres. Those relating to the Guide Book area and already published include the Black Mount, Glencoe, Mamores, Ben Nevis, Grey Corries, Moor of Rannoch and the Ben Alder group.

2½-inch O.S. (1:25,000). Although the country is being steadily covered from the far north southward, none of the sheets so far issued comes within the area of the Guide Book.

One-inch O.S. (Seventh Series). Indispensable whichever other maps are possessed or carried. The following are those applicable: No. 36 (Fort Augustus), No. 37 (Kingussie), No. 46 (Loch Linnhe), No. 47 (Glencoe), No. 48 (Loch Tay) and No. 53 (Loch Lomond).

One-inch O.S. Tourist Maps. Based on the ordinary one-inch O.S. In addition, however, to heights being shown by the usual line contours at a vertical interval of 50 ft., layer tints and hill shading give a readily understood impression of the topography. Of the three Scottish sheets only one – Ben Nevis and Glencoe – is applicable.

Bartholomew's Half-inch Maps. These maps, with contours at 250-ft. intervals and familiar colour-tinted layer system, are also thoroughly useful. The following sheets are applicable: No. 47 (Mull & Oban), No. 48 (Perthshire), and No. 51 (Grampians).

Accommodation

For those whose preference is for luxury and soft living the hand-books of the motoring associations and the Scottish Tourist Board's publication *Where to Stay in Scotland* will provide all the information necessary.

Youth Hostels. The following Youth Hostels are situated within the area of the Guide Book:

Cruachan. On the slopes of Ben Cruachan $\frac{1}{4}$ mile west of Loch Awe Station.

Glencoe. On the old road 1 mile south of Glencoe village.

Glen Nevis. On the south-west bank of the River Nevis, 3 miles from Fort William.

Loch Ossian. At the west end of Loch Ossian, 1 mile from Corrour Station. (Open, with warden, May–October; at other times by arrangement.)

Loch Lochy. On the main Fort William–Inverness road, between Loch Oich and Loch Lochy, 12 miles north of Spean Bridge.

Aviemore. On the main road at the south end of the village.

Kingussie. On the East Terrace, near the Clock Tower.

Club Huts. It should be noted that custodians named are those holding office in 1970. Charges presently range between 10p and 30p. 1s. 6d. and 6s. 0d., are not given.

Clashgour (Glasgow University). 1 mile west of Forest Lodge (NN 256425). 12 places, members or non-members. No keys at Forest Lodge. Postal applications, at least 10 days in advance, to: Hut Custodian, G.U.M. Club, c/o The Union, Glasgow University.

Black Rock (Ladies' Scottish Climbing Club). 1 mile south-east of Kingshouse Hotel, Glencoe (NN 268530). 10 places, L.S.C.C., members of clubs granting reciprocal rights, others as guests of L.S.C.C. members. Custodian: Miss P. Cain, Ayton House, Glenfarg, Perthshire.

Inbhirfhaolain (Grampian Club). $7\frac{1}{2}$ miles down Glen Etive (NN 158508). 11 places, plus outhouses; ample camping space. Available to members of clubs affiliated to M.C. of S. or B.M.C.; applications through club or meet secretaries to custodian: D. Green, 62 Glamis Road, Dundee.

Lagangarbh (S.M.C.). Altnafeadh, Glencoe (NN 221560). 18 places plus 4 for S.M.C. members. Permit letters authorizing kindred club parties must be obtained by club secretaries from custodian: D. E. Whitham, The Glen, Balerno, Midlothian.

Steall (J.M.C.S. Lochaber Section). Glen Nevis gorge (NN 178684). 15 places. Bookings to custodian: T. Corfield, Stobhan, Fassifern Road, Fort William.

Charles Inglis Clark Memorial Hut, Ben Nevis (S.M.C.). Allt a' Mhuilinn at 2200 feet just below Douglas Boulder (NN 168723). 16 places (minimum booking 3 places). Permit letters as for Lagangarbh from custodian: G. S. Peet, 6 Roman Way, Dunblane. Keys available also from: G. Tiso, 44 Rodney Street, Edinburgh; A. G. Cousins, 11 Kirklee Quadrant, Glasgow, W.2.; W. Robertson, 1 Montrose Square, Inverlochy, Fort William (password from custodian required).

Creag Meaghaidh (J.M.C.S. Glasgow Section). Coire Ardair, Creag Meaghaidh, at south-west corner of and some 200 feet above lochan (NN 435878). 6 places, bookable. Custodian: W. H. Duncan, 92 Fauldshead Road, Renfrew. Not to be used during stalking season, mid-August to mid-October.

Milehouse (L.S.C.C.). Near south-east corner of Loch Insh (NH 839044). 9 places, as for Black Rock. Bookings to club secretary: Miss L. W. Urquhart, 23 Keystone Quadrant, Milngavie.

Special mentions. The following may also be usefully mentioned:

Benalder Cottage. Alder Bay, Loch Ericht (NN 499680). Weatherproof, but no facilities. Excellent base for Ben Alder.

Creag Dubh. Good camping ground in broad, flat area of pastureland beside ponds and river, directly below the crags.

Mountain Rescue

Panels of volunteers for mountain rescue are maintained for help in various parts of Scotland by the mountaineering clubs in each area and can be called out if required. For the past few years also a great deal of the search and rescue in Scotland has been undertaken by the R.A.F. Mountain Rescue Teams from Kinloss and Leuchars, and their willing help is greatly appreciated; this does not, however, remove the obligation on all climbers in the vicinity to offer their help.

In the event of an accident, seek help at a mountain rescue post or the nearest police station, whichever is quicker.

The following are the mountain rescue posts for the Central Highlands area, with the names of supervisors and telephone numbers:

Glencoe and farther South –

Crianlarich Police Station	Officer in charge	Crianlarich 222
Kingshouse Hotel, Glencoe	Mr. MacDonald	Kingshouse 259
Scottish Ski Club, Meall a' Bhùiridh	Mr. R. E. Pender, 147 Bath Street, Glasgow, C.2.	
Clachaig Hotel, Glencoe	Mr. Macdonald	Ballachulish 252
Glencoe Mountain Rescue Team, Allt na Reigh, Glencoe	Mr. Hamish MacInnes, B.E.M.	Kingshouse 305 or Police 999

Glencoe. If seeking help the first call should be on Glencoe Mountain Rescue Team. The rescue kits in this area are kept at Clachaig Hotel at the west end of the glen and Kingshouse Hotel at the east end. There is a telephone at the Glen Etive road junction. There are 3 footbridges across the River Coe: (1) immediately below the junction of the Allt Coire Gabhail; (2) below Loch Achtriochtan; (3) behind. Clachaig Hotel. The best route from Buachaille Etive Mòr to Lagangarbh is over the summit and west along the ridge for $\frac{1}{2}$ mile to a col, from which easy slopes lead down to the hut, where there is a footbridge across the River Coupall.

Achnambeithach (West end of Loch Achtriochtan. NN 140566)	Mr. W. Elliot	Ballachulish 311 or Police 999
Fort William Police Station	Officer in charge	Ft. William 2361
C.I.C. Hut, Ben Nevis	Mr. A. Hill, 3 Glendessary Street, Caol, Fort William	
Steall Hut, Glen Nevis	Lochaber Mountaineering Club	

Ben Nevis. If seeking help, summon help through police at Fort William. There are 3 rescue kits in this area: at the C.I.C. Hut, at

Steall Hut and in Fort William. The best route off the mountain is down the track to the Glen Nevis Youth Hostel, where there is a telephone and which is accessible to motor transport. There is also a path from the C.I.C. Hut down the Allt a' Mhuilinn to the Fort William–Spean Bridge road. There are footbridges across the River Nevis at the Youth Hostel and at Steall. In ice conditions the descent into Coire Leis from the north-eastern ridge can be very dangerous (see Chapter 11 – Càrn Mòr Dearg). Keep the signposts on your left. A compass bearing alone may mislead. To safeguard the descent in difficult conditions, six abseil posts are fixed at 50-foot intervals leading down into the corrie (G.R. NN 171711). They are not way markers, but there for roping down. Shelters have been erected on Càrn Dearg, N.W. (NN 158719), the summit (NN 167713) and in Coire Leis (NN 174713).

Monadh Liath –

Cairngorm Mountain Rescue Team	Officer in charge, Police Station, Aviemore	Aviemore 222

It should be noted particularly that the position of a post is sometimes changed and should be verified locally.

Bibliography

Lists of books providing further information or of outstanding interest are given at the end of each chapter. To be noted particularly are the specialized S.M.C. rock-guides indispensable to those with more serious climbing plans.

Of general interest are *The Drove Roads of Scotland* by A. R. B. Haldane (Edinburgh University Press, 1968) and *The Highlands and Islands*, in the New Naturalist series, by F. Fraser Darling and J. Morton Boyd (Collins, 1964), while the Scottish Ski Club's booklet, *Ski-ing in Scotland*, and *Scottish Mountains on Ski*, Volume I, by Malcolm Slesser (West Col, 1970) are both invaluable to the ski-mountaineer.

Two classics of fiction, R. L. Stevenson's *Kidnapped* and *The New Road* by Neil Munro, add vivid background colour, and research among the 29 volumes of the *Scottish Mountaineering Club Journal* is always thoroughly rewarding.

Acknowledgements

First, to all those whose contributions of many different kinds went to the making of the indispensable, earlier editions of this Guide-Book; similarly to those who, since then, have gone on making and recording so much mountaineering history.

To Dr. W. F. H. Nicolaisen, Acting Head of the School of Scottish Studies, Edinburgh University, and his colleague on the Scottish Place-Name Survey, Mr. Ian A. Fraser, for having so kindly given help with expert interpretation of the Gaelic mountain names.

To Mr. Campbell Forrest for his contributions on the geology of the area and, more specifically, the Parallel Roads of Glen Roy, and to Mr. Alasdair McKeith for his description of the winter climbing routes on Creag Meaghaidh.

To Mr. George D. Banks and Mr. Hamish Mackinven of the North of Scotland Hydro-Electric Board's Information Staff for helpful details concerning the Awe Scheme.

To Mr. Philip Rankin, Managing Director of White Corries Ltd, for ski-ing fact and comment of much interest, mainly as regards Meall a' Bhùiridh.

More generally, but no less sincerely, to all those club members – S.M.C., J.M.C.S., Lochaber, L.S.C.C. – who have helped to check up on innumerable details and also who have so willingly contributed photographs.

And finally to Dr. Malcolm Slesser, General Guide Books Editor, who has acted as taskmaster with unfailing geniality and benevolence.

Ben Cruachan

(1) *Ben Cruachan (3689 ft.). Between Loch Awe and Loch Etive.
(2)   Stob Dearg (3611 ft.). $\frac{1}{2}$ mile W.N.W. of (1).
(3)   Meall Cuanail (3004 ft.). $\frac{1}{2}$ mile south of (1).
(4)   Drochaid Glas (3312 ft.). 1 mile east of (1).
(5) *Stob Diamh (3272 ft.). Mid-point of eastern horseshoe, $\frac{3}{4}$ mile E. by N. of (4).
(6)   Sròn an Isean (3163 ft.). $\frac{1}{3}$ mile E. by N. of (5).
(7)   Stob Garbh (3215 ft.). $\frac{1}{3}$ mile south of (5).
(8)   Beinn a' Bhùiridh (2941 ft.). $1\frac{1}{3}$ miles south of (5).

Ben Cruachan or, more correctly, Cruachan Beann, is one of the best known and most popular mountains in Scotland. In its magnificent situation above Loch Awe, where the latter, island-clustered, divides north-east to its head, north-west to the furrow of the Pass of Brander, it commands immediate attention; again and again from the Oban road to the west, from Loch Etive-side to the north and from innumerable hill-tops round about, its classic summit spires attract and hold the interest.

The whole extensive massif, beautifully wooded over parts of the lower slopes, occupies an area of some 20 square miles with the shape, roughly, of a parallelogram. Across this the actual backbone of the mountain, a switchback reaching 2 miles westwards from the mid-point of a deep horseshoe, provides one of the most familiar and most enjoyable ridge-walks on the mainland of Scotland.

Ben Cruachan and its surroundings have many historical and literary associations. There may be a good deal of misty obscurity about the exploits there of Sir William Wallace as narrated in the minstrel verses of 'Blind Harry', but there seems no doubt that in the Pass of Brander in 1308 King Robert the Bruce had his revenge for the earlier humiliation of Dalrigh by soundly defeating Macdougall of Lorn and his men. John Barbour, in his national epic *The Brus*, makes mention of 'Crechanben'.

It was on the good land at the foot of Glen Noe, on Loch Etive-side, that traditionally the original Macintyres settled, having crossed in their galley from Skye with their white cow. Holding office there as Foresters of Lorn for some 300 years, they paid an annual rent to the Campbells of a white calf and a midsummer snowball collected from the northern corries of Cruachan. Unwisely, however, at the beginning of the 18th century, they commuted this payment into money and when in due time the rent was increased, the ancestral home had to be sold.

At the head of Loch Awe, 'the river loch', the ruins of Kilchurn Castle stand picturesquely on a rocky platform projecting from a low, marshy peninsula. Dating probably from 1432, the castle was rebuilt and enlarged about 1615 and was the chief seat of the Breadalbane Campbells until they removed to Taymouth Castle nearly a century and a half later.

Also of great historical interest are the islands near the head of the loch – Innishail, with its ruined convent and chapel, Innis Chonnain, island of St. Connan, and Fraoch Eilean, on which stand the ruins of the ancient castle given into the keeping of the Mac-Naghtens by Alexander III in 1267. It is not surprising that in the golden age of tourism as many as three pleasure steamers were in service simultaneously on the loch and, with the ascent of Cruachan, featured prominently among the summer attractions of the West Highlands.

The date of the first recorded ascent of Ben Cruachan cannot be established with any certainty. Probably, however, it was one of a number of Scottish hills climbed in or shortly before 1772 in the interests of botany – although it is not in fact notably rich in flora. It is given a brief mention by Pennant in his *Tour in Scotland* of 1769 and slightly less cursorily in the *Statistical Account* of 1793. In 1811 Dr. John Macculloch, describing an ascent from Taynuilt of between nine and ten hours, found the climb 'tedious, but not difficult'.

The £24·5m. Awe Scheme of the North of Scotland Hydro-Electric Board, which has made more recent history, is a composite one of three sections: Inverawe and Nant, self-contained and conventional, and Cruachan, of more particular interest as the first large-scale pumped storage hydro-electric development in Scotland.

For Inverawe, water from Loch Awe is diverted at a barrage in the Pass of Brander into a tunnel 3½ miles long, leading to a surface power station near the mouth of the River Awe. The water level along a short section of the original river channel was raised to make it the same as that of the loch, notable provision being made at the same time for the conservation of the salmon for which the river is so famous. Near Inverawe House a salmon hatchery which can accommodate three million eggs has been provided for use by the Awe District Fishery Board.

For the Nant development, a system of aqueducts supplements the natural river-flow to Loch Nant by collecting water from other streams, thus helping to raise the level of the loch itself by 70 feet behind a gravity structure dam. The water is fed thence by way of a concrete-lined pressure tunnel to an underground power station, after which it discharges into Loch Awe.

For the Cruachan project – inaugurated by Her Majesty the Queen on October 15, 1965 – a massive-buttress type dam, its crest 1315 feet above sea level, was built across the Allt Cruachan in order to form a high-level storage reservoir in the main south-facing corrie of the mountain. At the same time the formation of the machine hall – the major constructional work – was carried out by excavating out of the solid granite a vast subterranean cavern nearly 300 feet long and as high as a seven-storey building. In this hall – reached by a 1200-yard access tunnel running downhill from Loch Awe at a gradient of 1 in 20 – were housed the four combined pump-turbine units, each of 100 megawatts capacity. Power is brought to Cruachan during off-peak periods from thermal stations in south and east Scotland by way of the Windyhill substation on the outskirts of Glasgow and makes possible the forcing back of the water up the tunnels and shafts to the high-level reservoir.

An access road to the dam leaves the main A85 ¾ mile west of Loch Awe Hotel. This road is open to walkers, but because the hillside above the main road is so steep, great care must be taken not to dislodge stones which might cause interference to car traffic or on the railway line. The road is open to authorised vehicles only. During the summer daily bus tours to the scheme, including the dam, are run from Oban.

Two other stretches of the Board's roads may on occasion be found useful. The first of these, from the dam, follows the shore round the west side of the reservoir to its head. The second, also from the dam, contours the shoulder of Meall Cuanail for ¾ mile, then as a track, provided with marker posts, leads to an intake building on the Allt Brander.

Yet another recently constructed road – running to Glennoe Farm

25

1. Ben Cruachan. Stob Dearg and Main Peak.

from near Inverawe House – may prove useful to those wishing to explore the north side of the mountain. The road is private and unsuitable for ordinary cars, but there is no objection to its use by those on foot and permission may be obtained from the farm (Taynuilt 212).

Ben Cruachan, Main Peak (3689 ft.) – Undoubtedly the best way to appreciate Cruachan to the full is to take in all seven tops in a single ridge-walk, an expedition which involves approximately 6000 feet of ascent. Either direction is enjoyable, although an east to west choice allows the most to be made of the far views down Loch Awe and towards the islands, for which the mountain is celebrated.

The time-honoured approach to the main peak itself is by way of the Falls of Cruachan. From the former Falls railway station a poor path climbs steeply up slopes beautifully wooded with oak and hazel and birch, on the west bank of the Allt Cruachan, and leads eventually to the access road to the dam – a point which may of course be reached, possibly with less exertion, by following the gentler 3 miles of the road itself. From the head of the reservoir an ascent may be made leftwards by the burn to the Cuanail-Cruachan bealach. This route, however, is shut in and steep, and it is preferable to go over **Meall Cuanail** itself (3004 ft.). The drop from that top to the col is only 200 ft. and an easy climb thereafter leads to the summit (triangulation point).

From Taynuilt, Cruachan is usually climbed by way of Stob Dearg, but a direct route may be taken from the main road at the Awe barrage. The burn which comes down 150 yards south-east of the lay-by or else the more deeply cut Allt Brander may be followed steeply upwards until the gradient eases. It is then better to choose the gentle slopes to the Cuanail-Cruachan bealach than to make directly up the slabby corrie-face ahead.

The north ridge to the summit is not steep except for the final few feet, but it is pleasantly narrow and forms the best route of approach from Glen Noe.

When leaving the summit in thick weather, care should be taken not to miss the line of the main ridge. Towards Stob Dearg the route for the first few yards is the same as to Meall Cuanail then west to the saddle; eastwards, towards Drochaid Glas, the ridge is at first narrow and steep.

Stob Dearg (3611ft.) – The fact that this, the 'Taynuilt Peak' so well seen from the west, is only slightly lower than the summit itself explains why distant views are frequently of the 'twin peaks of Cruachan'. The usual approach from Taynuilt is by the Allt Cruin-iche, ½ mile south-east of Bridge of Awe. The burn should be followed to the upper corrie and the top reached by the S.S.W. ridge. From the 'Taynuilt Peak' the ridge to the main summit is quite easy.

In summer some fair rock-scrambling may be had on Stob Dearg, on the granite slabs facing north-west and north, while under winter conditions the north ridge can give an exhilarating snow and ice climb. In March 1892 (J. H. Gibson, W. R. Lester, W. Douglas and Macindoe) and again in January 1936 (J. H. B. Bell, D. Myles and A. Maclure) it required several hours of step-cutting.

Drochaid Glas (3312 ft.) – In coming east from the summit the ridge swings round northwards to reach this narrow, rocky top. In mist the climber may easily miss the main ridge here as it really disappears entirely, the continuation eastwards lying down a steep slope of scree and boulders. On a number of occasions parties have carried on over Drochaid Glas, on which there is no cairn, and found themselves descending the steep and narrow north ridge into Glen Noe. To reach the next top, Stob Diamh, one should descend to the east 20 yards short of the top of Drochaid Glas. The north ridge gives a good scramble of 200 ft. and at least one snow gully has been climbed on the north-east face. The latter has also been descended by gullies and ledges, but the rock-climbing on it is not satisfactory.

Stob Diamh (3272 ft.) – has been ranked as a separate mountain in view of its distance from the main summit and the fact that it is the highest point of the eastern 'horseshoe'.

From it ridges run out E. by N. to **Sròn an Isean** (3163 ft.), with a dip of 300 ft., and south to **Stob Garbh** (3215 ft.), dip 250 ft. Some 500 yards south of the latter the ridge divides and the curve of the 'horseshoe' drops away to the moor.

To make the circuit of these eastern tops the main road should be left at the Stronmilchan fork, ¾ mile from Loch Awe Hotel, and the track north over the moor – formerly the small-gauge railway line to the old lead mines – followed for nearly 2 miles round into Coire Ghlais. The burn from the latter may be crossed by a decrepit bridge just above its junction with the Allt Coire Chreachainn at a height of 500 ft., and from here the 'horseshoe' may be ascended easily to the main ridge and Stob Garbh. The descent from Stob Diamh to Sròn an Isean is steep at first and might be missed in bad weather if care is not taken, while the lowest section of the descent from the Sròn to the moor is over fairly steep grass.

Beinn a' Bhùiridh (2941 ft.) is the final top of the ridge which runs south from Stob Garbh, the intervening bealach being known as the Larig Torran. The descent of 500 ft. to the latter from the flat summit plateau of Beinn a' Bhùiridh is quite steep and under winter conditions is often iced.

Beinn a' Bhùiridh's north face, which extends along the out-thrust shoulder of Monadh Driseig and overlooks the Allt Coire Ghlais, is rocky and seamed by gullies. Two or three of the latter have been climbed, but the only route recorded in any detail dates from January 1905. To the east of a prominent rock-bluff – reached by working diagonally upwards from about 1 mile above the bridge over the Allt Coire Ghlais – a short length of cliff is cut by two well-defined gullies. Between these is a crack or chimney affording a climb of three pitches, rather wet and grassy in places (W. A. Morrison, T. E. Goodeve and A. E. Robertson).

A number of other routes, mostly lacking in recorded details, have been enjoyed at this eastern end of Cruachan. Some rock-scrambling may be had on the north face of Stob Diamh and on the east face of Stob Garbh, while the latter's prominent south-east buttress gave an interesting snow-climb in January 1939 (I. G. Jack, C. R. and C. M. Steven). Sròn an Isean has been climbed more than once from the north, for example in January 1928 by way of an iced gully with several pitches (Martin, A. G. Smith, T. E. Thomson and J. P. Watson) and again in December 1950 by a 600-foot gully involving a 30-foot ice pitch (I. G. Charleson, J. E. MacEwen, W. A. W. Russell, J. D. B. Wilson and W. Turner).

BIBLIOGRAPHY

A Progress in Mountaineering. J. H. B. Bell.
(Oliver and Boyd, 1950.) (North Ridge of Stob Dearg.)

2

Beinn Eunaich Group

(1) ***Beinn a' Chochuill** (3215 ft.). 3½ miles N. by W. of Loch Awe Hotel.
(2) ***Beinn Eunaich** (3242 ft.). 1½ miles east of (1).
(3) **Beinn Mhic-Mhonaidh** (2602 ft.). 5¾ miles N.N.E. of Dalmally Station.

Ben Cruachan's close neighbours to the north-east, Beinn a' Cho-chuill and Beinn Eunaich, form the culminating points of a well-defined ridge which climbs steadily for 5 miles from the shore of Loch Etive. In themselves they lack Cruachan's outstanding char-acter – the dominant position and the distinctive architecture of peak and corrie, attractive no matter the season of the year. To be at their best these two hills need crisp winter conditions, when their summits and the ridge which links them can provide an enjoyable expedition with a fine range of views.

They derive nevertheless a special interest from the glens which are essentially a part of their make-up – not so much Glen Strae, the rather barren south-west to north-east boundary, as Glen Noe, Glen Liever, and Glen Kinglass, dropping in parallel to Loch Etive. These three, among the least accessible and least often explored in Scotland, are well seen as one sails up Loch Etive – unfortunately not so easily enjoyed now that the classic summer cruises have come to an end with the sale of the popular launch *Etive Shearwater*. Further exploration is invited, one way perhaps by following the public track which leads right through Glen Kinglass to Loch Tulla, 14 miles away. Certainly the pleasures of Glen Kinglass have a way of being particularly seductive, at least one party having been be-guiled by its fine rock-pools into lazing away a hot summer day instead of climbing Beinn a' Chochuill, as intended, from the north.

Beinn a' Chochuill (3215 ft.) – If climbed on its own, the usual route is, of course, from the south, from Dalmally or Loch Awe, by way of the Allt Mhoille. A Hydro-Board road, for Land-Rovers only and scarring the west flank of Beinn Eunaich high above the glen, runs from Castles Farm to a hut built by the Board at a point $\frac{1}{3}$ mile short of and 400 ft. below the Sròn an Isean–Beinn a' Chochuill bealach, the Larig Noe. At about 1200 ft. a short branch road breaks away sharply to the right across Beinn a' Chochuill's south-east ridge and the latter may then be followed without difficulty to the top of the shoulder above, $\frac{1}{2}$ mile from the summit. Alternatively it may be preferred to shun the road altogether and reach the highest point of the pass by the track to the Cruachan 'horseshoe' and up to the west side of the Allt Mhoille. From the bealach 1400 ft. of fairly steep grass and scree lead up an ill-defined ridge, past a small south-east facing corrie, to the summit.

On the north side of the summit ridge the slopes dropping to the head of Glen Liever are steep but not precipitous.

More often Beinn a' Chochuill is climbed from Beinn Eunaich by way of the easy east-west ridge, the lowest point of which is 2350 ft. From this saddle a 500-ft. shoulder and gentler rise for $\frac{3}{4}$ mile lead to the Beinn a' Chochuill cairn.

Beinn Eunaich (3242 ft.) – Well seen in views from the head of Loch Awe, Beinn Eunaich is easily climbed by its south ridge, the prominent nose of which is named Stob Maol. From Castles Farm, ignoring the blandishments of the Hydro-Board road, it is best to outflank the steep lowest section of the Stob by working round to the east, where gentler slopes of moor-grass give access to the broad shoulder above. A gradual ascent then leads to the junction of two indeterminate ridges 200 yards short of the summit cairn.

The main west ridge to Beinn a' Chochuill, mentioned above, drops 900 ft. to the saddle, while the north-east ridge to the outlier Meall Copagach (2656 ft.) descends more steeply for about 600 ft., then, continuing narrow and well-defined, passes over an intermediate unnamed top of 2800 ft. At Meall Copagach the ridge swings east to Beinn Lurachain (2346 ft.) across the saddle over which runs a path from Glen Strae to Glen Kinglass.

Two climbs which feature noteworthily in the early history of the S.M.C. – the Black and the White Shoot – are located on a steep rock outcrop prominent on the south-east ridge of Beinn Eunaich. To reach this outcrop the forestry road up Glen Strae should be followed for 1 mile, then left in favour of an indistinct path branching off 100 yards beyond the end of the plantation and just short of a conspicuous pyramid-shaped moraine on the right. This path – the route to Glen Kinglass over the Meall Copagach–Beinn Lurachain col – is followed for another ¾ mile to within sight of the outcrop. The climbs themselves lie farther round and come into view when one has contoured the lower ridge and arrived directly below them.

The Black Shoot. 300 ft. Very difficult. (J. H. Gibson, W. W. Naismith, W. R. Lester and W. Douglas. May 1892.) The climb begins at a height of 1750 ft. up a 'somewhat ill-defined water-slide, a mossy luzula-bedecked wall of very considerable steepness'. This can be avoided by way of the buttress on the right, up a narrow ledge, round a delicate balance corner, then a traverse back into the Shoot above the water-slide. A short, mossy pitch, climbed on the left wall, is followed by easier ground and then the more strenuous 'Twisted Chimney'. Thereafter the direct route leads to a sloping ledge on the right wall and easy scrambling beyond.

The White Shoot. (J. H. Gibson, F. Campbell, W. R. Lester and R. A. Robertson. March 1891.) An easier gully to the right of the Black Shoot. About 200 ft. up the party traversed into an adjacent gully to the right and finished up a fine chimney.

Beaver Buttress. 400 ft. Difficult. (J. H. B. Bell, J. Rooke Corbett, C. W. Parry and A. P. A. Robertson. December 1927.) Between the two gullies just described. A vertical corner of 10 ft. with an upward traverse to the left enables the party to look down into the Black Shoot above the first pitch. Trending right by way of narrow ledges, with no abundance of belays, an awkward chimney is crossed and higher to the right a ledge is gained, this time overlooking the White Shoot. The finish is by two 15-ft. pitches, severe on the first ascent under conditions of hard frost and powder snow but reckoned as probably difficult in summer. Above is easier ground and scrambling to the top of the buttress.

North-East Gully. 350 ft. (D. Scott and R. Anderson. February 1946.) In the north-east corrie of Beinn Eunaich, a snow and ice climb up a succession of steep rocks and gullies. At the lowest point on the north side of the main upper cliffs a start was made in a gully south of a prominent ridge with a striking pinnacle.

From here a route was worked out partly in the gully and partly on a rib of rock and leading finally to the summit ridge about 15 yards north of the cairn.

Beinn Mhic-Mhonaidh (2602 ft.), wedge-shaped and isolated, stands out prominently in views up Glen Strae. If approached by way of the latter, the forestry road will be found helpful till it ends after 2 miles. Thereafter the long south-west ridge, steep at two-thirds height, is the obvious choice of route. The approach from Glen Orchy has a potentially interesting start, as the bridge across the river $\frac{1}{4}$ mile south of the Allt Broighleachan junction is stoutly defended by a locked gate and barbed wire, and might only 'go' as a result of some determined hand-traversing. From a bothy on the west side of the Orchy a path (not marked on the one-inch O.S. map) leads to and along the nearer bank of the Allt Broighleachan to within $\frac{1}{2}$ mile of the wood that is shown, but neither the route nor the climb beyond have any great merit.

3

Ben Starav Group

---

(1) *Beinn nan Aighean (3141 ft.). 8 miles west of Forest Lodge, Loch Tulla.
(2) *Ben Starav (3541 ft.). 1¾ miles S. by E. of Loch Etive Head.
(3)   Meall Cruidh (3049 ft.). ⅔ mile S. by E. of (2).
(4)   Stob Coire Dheirg (3372 ft.). ⅓ mile east of (2).
(5) *Glas Bheinn Mhòr (3258 ft.). 1¾ miles east of (2).
(6) *Stob Coir' an Albannaich (3425 ft.). 1⅓ miles north-east of (5).
(7) *Meall nan Eun (3039 ft.). 1½ miles E. by N. of (6).

This compact group, culminating in the fine peak of Ben Starav, is bounded by the upper reaches of Loch Etive, by the 9-mile crescent of Glen Kinglass and by the high pass, running roughly north-west and south-east, formed by the Allt Ceitlein and the Allt Dochard. Composed mainly of granite, the mountains tend to have steep grassy slopes facing south and west, with their north and east sides bold and craggy. From the north the group is readily accessible from lower Glen Etive; in the east the best starting-point is Forest Lodge, a mile past Inveroran.

In cattle-droving days Inveroran was one of the regular stances on the route from Skye and Lochaber to the great trysts of Crieff and – after the middle of the eighteenth century – Falkirk. It was in the old thatched inn there that Dorothy and William Wordsworth, southward bound on their Highland tour, stopped for breakfast on a September morning in 1803. Coming from Kingshouse, they had been interested to see near Loch Tulla a great herd of cattle, 'a stream coursing the road, with off-stragglers to the borders of the lake and under the trees on the sloping ground.' Later in the kitchen of the inn they saw seven or eight drovers with their dogs. Unfortunately for the travellers, however, their breakfast was not one to inspire equally happy memories: 'The butter not eatable, the barley-cakes fusty, the oatbread so hard I could not chew it, and there were only four eggs in the house, which they had boiled as hard as stones.'

By the early days of the S.M.C. times had changed vastly and several highly successful meets were held at Inveroran – the first of these in May 1897 – and there is, of course, an inn still there today.

Beinn nan Aighean (3141 ft.) – or, as given on the one-inch map, Beinn nan Aighenan – is the most remote and probably the least often visited of the group. It may, however, be worked pleasantly into a crossing of some 14 miles from Loch Tulla to the head of Loch Etive. The route of approach from Forest Lodge follows the public track which leads through to Glen Kinglass and Loch Etive. After skirting the south shore of Loch Dochard and walking over almost 2 miles of moorland, the river should be crossed by the bridge at the map spot-height 617 ft. (Grid Reference: NN 185403) and the main east ridge of Beinn nan Aighean climbed to its outlying 2400-ft. top. Thence a walk of 1 mile, with a wide range of views, leads easily to the summit.

An alternative approach of comparable length may be made from Loch Awe or Dalmally. This entails, however, the crossing of the 2000-ft. Meall Copagach–Beinn Lurachain bealach and it may be felt that a brief taste of the remote higher reaches of Glen Kinglass, pleasant though these may be, is insufficient compensation for so much toil. The choice thereafter – likely to be decided by the height of the Kinglass – is whether to continue upstream and cross the river by the bridge near the Lodge, or to ford it and follow a useful path beside the Allt Hallater up the steep lower slopes of Beinn nan Aighean.

The ridge running N. by W. from the summit to meet the main ridge between Ben Starav and Glas Bheinn Mhòr drops at its lowest point to 2000 ft.

Ben Starav (3541 ft.). – Rising steeply from the head of Loch Etive, this fine peak is justly popular. It is a big mountain and its graceful summit is the culminating point of five ridges – north, east, south-east, south-west and north-west – in places narrow and, under snow, often beautifully corniced.

Ben Starav is usually climbed from the head of Loch Etive, a start being made conveniently at the bridge to Coileitir Farm. From here the very pleasant north ridge – often the nesting territory of ptarmigan in late spring – is reached by a second bridge, across the Allt Mheuran, and leads in another 2 miles to the summit.

From the head of Loch Etive a good snow climb up the northern

corrie was enjoyed in April 1949 (M. B. Nettleton) and other winter routes might be worth investigating there.

The mountain may also be approached from Inveroran in the east, possibly as climax to the crossing to Loch Etive over Beinn nan Aighean.

Meall Cruidh (3049 ft.) is named only on the six-inch map, being indicated on the one-inch by contour-line on the south-east ridge just after the latter turns south. A swing south-west follows to yet another small top, then west to Stob an Duine Ruaidh (2624 ft.). From here a descent may be made to Loch Etive – as it may similarly by Ben Starav's south-west ridge direct from the summit – but it should be noted that the path along the loch-side shown on the map is poor enough to make the 4 miles back to Coileitir seem doubly long and tedious.

Stob Coire Dheirg (3372 ft.) – The main easterly ridge of Starav runs at first for 300 yards south-east to the head of the fine south-east corrie. It then turns north-east in a narrow section which sometimes forms a beautiful snow arête, and in about $\frac{1}{3}$ mile rises to Stob Coire Dheirg, another top named only on the six-inch map. The ridge then drops E.S.E. to about 2500 ft., where the ridge from Beinn nan Aighean comes in, before climbing gradually eastwards once again to Glas Bheinn Mhòr.

Glas Bheinn Mhòr (3258 ft.) – This hill is well seen from Glen Etive, rising dome-shaped from its east and west ridges. It is easily approached from Coileitir Farm up the Allt Mheuran, then by the long northern spur which joins the west ridge $\frac{1}{2}$ mile from the summit – a route which avoids the tedious screes of the north face. Like Ben Starav, Glas Bheinn Mhòr may also of course be reached from Inveroran.

Stob Coir' an Albannaich (3425 ft.) – This is the prominent peak seen from Loch Tulla, looking up Glen Dochard. The top is the highest point of a long ridge running north-west from two spurs overlooking Loch Dochard, Cùil Ghlas and Sròn na h-Iolaire, while its north-west shoulder, Beinn Chaorach, drops down to Glen Etive.

2. *Opposite :* Ben Cruachan and Loch Etive, from Ben Starav. In the far distance the Paps of Jura.

As with its neighbours, the alternative routes of approach are from Coileitir Farm or else from Inveroran.

Some careful map-reading is advisable if the way to Glas Bheinn Mhòr is to be found in mist: first south of west, then east of south, before turning south-west to gain the ridge to Glas Bheinn Mhòr.

On Beinn Chaorach the compact granite crag of Creag Chaorach faces south-east towards Stob Coir' an Albannaich; it is clearly seen in profile from the summit of Buachaille Etive Mòr. The best approach is to follow Glen Ceitlein till it forks, then scramble up the gorge into the corrie between Stob Coir' an Albannaich and Beinn Chaorach, passing a striking pinnacle on the way. A well-defined area of cracks and deep V-grooves divides the crag into two portions: to the left of these faults is an expanse of steep slabs, to the right are three narrow buttresses. The leftmost buttress has a striking pink slab, capped by a line of overhangs. The two routes reported lie on this buttress. The rock is sound and nowhere difficult.

Central Rib. 400 ft. Difficult. (J. R. Marshall and R. N. Campbell. April 1967). The line of least resistance, finishing up the rib bounding the pink slab on the right.

Eezay Edge. 350 ft. Severe. (J. Brumfitt and B. Sproul. May 1967.) Follow the left edge of the buttress throughout.

Patey's Old Man. 70 ft. Unclassifiable. (I. Rowe and B. Sproul. May 1967.) The striking pinnacle mentioned above. It protrudes from the left wall of the gorge. Lasso the top and climb the rope. Treat gently.

Meall nan Eun (3039 ft.) is a rather featureless flat-topped mountain, although steep-sided on east and south. From Glen Etive the easiest line of approach lies up the Allt Ceitlein to its source between Meall Tarsuinn (2871 ft.) and Meall nan Eun, and thence to the latter's north-west ridge. On the other side of the mountain a path from the west end of Loch Dochard may be followed over the moor towards the glen of the Allt Dochard's north-western tributary, then a suitable route picked out up the rather steep and slabby face above.

More often than not, however, Meall nan Eun is linked with its neighbour, Stob Coir' an Albannaich, to make a single expedition that can have in it a fuller measure of interest.

4

The Black Mount

(1) ***Stob Ghabhar** (3565 ft.). $3\frac{1}{4}$ miles north-west of Forest Lodge, Loch Tulla.
(2) ***Stob a' Choire Odhair** (3058 ft.). $1\frac{3}{4}$ miles E. by N. of (1).
(3) **Aonach Eagach** (3272 ft.). $\frac{1}{3}$ mile E.S.E. of (1).
(4) **Sròn a' Ghearrain** (3240 ft.). $\frac{1}{3}$ mile W. by N. of (1).
(5) **Stob a' Bhruaich Lèith** (3083 ft.). $1\frac{1}{2}$ miles W. by N. of (1).
(6) **Sròn nan Giubhas** (3174 ft.). $\frac{1}{2}$ mile north of (1).
(7) ***Clach Leathad** (3602 ft.). 1 mile south-west of (9).
(8) **Mam Coire Easain** (3506 ft.). $\frac{1}{2}$ mile north of (7).
(9) ***Meall a' Bhùiridh** (3636 ft.). $2\frac{3}{4}$ miles S. by W. of Kingshouse Hotel.
(10) **Crèise** (3600 ft.). $\frac{1}{2}$ mile north of (8).
(11) **Stob a' Ghlais Choire** (3207 ft.). $\frac{1}{2}$ mile north of (10).
(12) **Beinn Mhic Chasgaig** (2820 ft.). $1\frac{1}{4}$ miles W.N.W. of (7).
(13) **Beinn Ceitlein, Stob Dubh** (2897 ft.). $1\frac{1}{2}$ miles south of Dalness, Glen Etive.

This magnificent range is usually referred to as the Black Mount, although the forest of that name also includes the Ben Starav group. Beautifully situated on the western borders of the Moor of Rannoch, it is well seen both from the main road crossing the Moor to Glencoe and, more distantly, from the railway. The southern slopes of Stob Ghabhar under snow, viewed from among the pines of the old Caledonian forest beside Loch Tulla, or again the huge sweep of ridge and corrie from Stob a' Choire Odhair to Meall a' Bhùiridh seen from Loch Bà, are among the finest mountain prospects in Argyll.

From Stob Ghabhar in the south to Sròn na Crèise in the north is $4\frac{1}{2}$ miles by the map, the ridge dropping only once below 2500 ft., at the Bealach Fùar-chathaidh (2320 ft.), between Aonach Mòr and Clach Leathad. For long the traverse of this ridge from Forest Lodge to Kingshouse has been one of the classic high-level expeditions of the district; more recently in the reverse direction from Meall a' Bhùiridh, it has come to be recognized as a supremely enjoyable *tour de force* for the skier.

Stob Ghabhar (3565 ft.) lies to the north-west of Loch Tulla and is most easily approached from Forest Lodge. The public track to Glen Kinglass and Loch Etive should be followed for 1 mile – with a section of rough boulders and three fords, not recommended for ordinary cars – to the Glasgow University Mountaineering Club's hut at Clashgour. The latter – not to be confused with the Clashgour cottage shown on the one-inch O.S. map and another 1¼ miles farther west – is the former school-house. Now as a club hut its sleeping capacity is nominally 12, with room for more at a pinch – a little perplexing perhaps to the visitor who contemplates it from the outside and discovers that its measurements are approximately 13 ft. by 11 ft.

At the hut a well-made subsidiary track turns off up the Allt Toaig, ascending gradually and contouring the slopes of Beinn Toaig and Stob a' Choire Odhair, then cutting back to zigzag up the shoulder of the latter. This path should be left at the 1000-ft. contour and a way made more steeply up to the corrie-lip beside the burn which comes down in a series of fine cascades – in high summer a country of much grass and many thirsty clegs. From above the falls the rusty fence running leftwards and up the south-east ridge may be found a useful guide, crossing the summit rocks of the mountain within 20 yards of the cairn. The E.S.E. ridge – Aonach Eagach – which forms the other arm of the corrie, is not recommended on account of its steep, blunt nose.

The final ridge of Stob Ghabhar is well defined, with steep rocks and scree falling to the great eastern corrie and more gentle slopes to the west.

The Upper Couloir. 300 ft. Grade II. (A. E. Maylard and three friends. May 1897.) In the eastern corrie, the rock buttress immediately below the cairn is split from top to bottom by a steep gully. This, in summer, contains at mid-height an objectionably slimy water-slide of about 100 ft., but under winter conditions gives a magnificent snow and ice climb – the classic Upper Couloir of Stob Ghabhar. The first pitch is usually snowed up and relatively easy, but above it the snow steepens and leads to the well-known ice-pitch – usually some 20–25 ft. of high-angle ice. Above this again steep snow leads to the summit ridge within a few yards of the cairn.

Upper Couloir Keyhole. 300 ft. Grade III. (C. L. Donaldson and G. J. Dutton. March 1952.) A slightly harder winter route a short

3. Stob Ghabhar from Loch Tulla.

distance to the right of the Upper Couloir, a narrow, deep-cut
gully rising from the left corner of a rock-bay. Steep snow leads
to a high-angled 20-ft. wall below a heavily iced chimney, then a
stretch of 100 ft. of ice, thinly masked in places with snow (thread
belay above). This is followed by further steep snow, whence a
sharp little ice arête leads downwards into the Upper Couloir
itself above the ice-pitch.

Hircine Rib. 350 ft. Severe. (P. Mitchell, J. Morrison and J. R.
Ewing. May 1961.) The buttress bounding the Upper Couloir on

41

the left. The rock is fine-grained, riven into vertical furrows and loose in places, with mainly outsloping holds and scant belays. Start at lowest rocks just right of centre and move up slightly leftwards, with the angle gradually increasing. At 90 ft. an awkward sloping ledge is reached, whence a difficult, smooth groove is climbed left of a rotten, undercut rib. Belay at 120 feet. A further 70-ft. section, started by an airy corner, is followed by 200 ft. of scrambling.

To reach these climbs, the bealach (2240 ft.) 1 mile east of the summit of Stob Ghabhar should be crossed and the slopes beyond contoured into the eastern corrie. Above the lochan and slightly to the right of a direct line between it and the summit, is the Lower Couloir, running up easily to a snowfield through some rocky outcrops. From the snowfield the summit ridge can be reached without difficulty by keeping to the right well clear of the rock-defences. The climb from the lochan to the summit by way of the two couloirs is 1340 ft., of which the Upper Couloir is about 300 ft.

Stob a' Choire Odhair (3058 ft.) is a separate 'Munro' lying $1\frac{3}{4}$ miles due east of Stob Ghabhar. If climbed on its own from Forest Lodge, use should be made of the path up the Allt Toaig and its south-west spur; if, however, it is climbed from Stob Ghabhar, the latter's **Aonach Eagach** ridge should be followed to just beyond its narrow notch and top (3272 ft.), then slopes of mixed scree, rock and grass descended to the col, after which there is an easy re-ascent of 850 ft.

Westwards from just beyond the summit of Stob Ghabhar an undulating ridge descends gradually for almost 3 miles to the outlying shoulder of Meall Odhar (2875 ft.). There are two tops on this ridge, first **Sròn a' Ghearrain** (3240 ft.) at $\frac{1}{3}$ mile, then, 1 mile farther on beyond a slightly more pronounced 150-ft. dip, **Stob a' Bhruaich Lèith** (3083 ft.). Most helpfully the broken-down fence continues along the broad, grassy approach to Sròn a' Ghearrain. Neither of the corries on the flanks of the ridge has any outstanding merit, although at the back of that on the left (south) is a narrow, square-cut couloir:

H. P. Gully. 300 ft. Grade I–II. (D. J. Pullin and B. T. Hill.

4. Coire Bà.

April 1967.) There may be an ice-pitch and the finish, a short
distance south of the cairn of the Sròn, is steep.

Continuing to Stob a' Bhruaich Lèith, one crosses a shallow grassy
depression, a south-facing sun-trap where in summer many hinds
and their calves may be seen, and sometimes heard. There are fine
views northwards to the Glencoe hills – notably of all three tops of
Buachaille Etive Mòr with the Dalness Chasm showing prominently.

Stob Ghabhar's fifth top, **Sròn nan Giubhas** (3174 ft.) takes its
name from the nose which separates the deep eastern corrie from

43

Coire Bà. It drops steeply and provides an enjoyable return route to Forest Lodge – from it across the corrie-mouth below the lochan, over the low Stob a' Choire Odhair bealach and so down the Allt Toaig path back to Clashgour.

Beyond the junction of the Sròn nan Giubhas shoulder the main ridge continues north-westwards in the long, straight line of Aonach Mòr – a delightful stairway of knolls and hollows, in summer of wheatears and meadow-pipits, and in sunshine of far views out across Rannoch Moor. In mist, however, it is not easy to hit off the point at which the route drops away north-eastwards from this spur into the dip of the Bealach Fùar-chathaidh. A false ridge quite early on must be avoided and the descent continued for ¾ mile to the lowest depression before the gentle re-ascent to Point 2839 ft. Some 200 yards beyond this dip one may at last turn off on the easy descent to the saddle.

Clach Leathad, or Clachlet (3602 ft.), the next important summit, gives its name to all the remainder of the range. It is a fine mountain viewed from the south-east, with the dark recesses of Coire Bà deep-set between its east ridge and the sharply-defined Sròn nan Giubhas. There is also a west ridge and this is joined 1000 feet above the Bealach Fùar-chathaidh after a stiff pull. Clachlet can also, of course, be climbed conveniently on its own from Bà Bridge on the old Glencoe road. Access to Bà Bridge by car is not possible from the north, but from the south the 4 miles of the road from Forest Lodge have been reasonably well maintained and may be used, outwith the stalking season and with permission.

Mam Coire Easain (3506 ft.), ½ mile north of the main summit of Clachlet, is not a particularly distinctive top, but it is important as the junction of the ridge to Beinn Mhic Chasgaig in the west and the slope which falls away steeply to link with the ridge of Meall a' Bhùiridh in the east.

Meall a' Bhùiridh (3636 ft.) is the highest summit of the Clachlet group and lies ¾ mile to the east of the main ridge, the lowest point of the intervening dip being 3070 ft.

Along with Ben Lawers, the Cairngorms and Glenshee, Meall a' Bhùiridh is one of the main ski-ing centres in Scotland. Its north-facing slopes have remarkable snow-holding properties and, with

1350 feet of uplift, offer the most interesting downhill running in the country.

The first recorded expedition there, by a party of the Ladies' Scottish Climbing Club, dates from as long ago as October 1917, but it was not until 1951 that the slopes attracted the attention of the Scottish Ski Club, prospecting at that time for a 'new' area suitable for mechanization. After four years of careful assessment, the club erected a tow on the top 900 ft. of the mountain. This was followed in 1959 by the formation of Scotland's first commercial company, White Corries Ltd, a chairlift being put up by the latter the following year and a second tow three years later, in 1963. The chairlift, it may be noted, now operates in summer as well as in winter, weather permitting.

The short access road from the A82, almost opposite Kingshouse Hotel, leads to a fairly adequate car-park and thence to a small tea-room beside the chairlift. Beyond the top of the latter (2090 ft.), extensive plateau slopes provide a variety of easy runs, not perhaps appreciated as much as they might be, on account of the attractions higher up and as they have not had the advantages of shelters or snow husbandry by drift fences. The majority of visiting skiers choose instead the 700-yard walk across the plateau from the chair-lift to the two upper tows, which together provide a further lift of 1350 vertical ft.

With the accent placed so strongly on mechanization, Meall a' Bhùiridh is essentially for the more efficient downhill only enthusiast and shares with the other main ski-ing centres in the various events of the Scottish racing calendar. The principal runs – Flypaper, Spring Run, Rannoch Glade, Massacre and West End – are all of a high standard of difficulty, although some are nevertheless within the powers of the moderate performer. The minimum 'straight' descent is roughly 1400 yards on a very fast race line, usually with a gentler run-out available to the chairlift. At the height of a good season it is possible to ski right down to the bottom of the chairlift, a distance of 2 miles with a drop of 2400 ft. – claimed to be the longest and, by not a few, the most enjoyable run in Scotland.

Several variation descents, possibly with more appeal to the ski-mountaineer, may be made from Meall a' Bhùiridh. From the eastern end of the summit plateau the descent of the east shoulder is a superb run, the most challenging on the mountain. Alternatively, after the walk round the ridge to Clachlet – with due care for the Coire

Easain cornices – another long descent may be had, also to ruined Bà Cottage, whence however the homeward trek is likely to be found tedious. Again, if snow conditions on the west side of the Creag Dhubh ridge are known to be good, a first-class diversion may be had down into Cam Ghleann of Sròn na Crèise, with a reasonable walk back to the Glen Etive road near Coupall Bridge.

Crèise (3600 ft.) – This top is not named on either the one-inch or the six-inch map. The height '3596' on the one-inch is 300 yards north of the 3600-ft. contour and the actual height is probably just a little over 3600 ft. Beyond it the ridge narrows, with rocky outcrops on both sides.

Stob a' Ghlais Choire (3207 ft.) – This bold top, with its projecting northerly shoulder, Sròn na Crèise (2952 ft.), presents a magnificent face towards Kingshouse, particularly fine when plastered thickly with new snow and looking decidedly steeper than it is.

5. On the Happy Valley run, Meall a' Bhùiridh. Mamores and Ben Nevis in the background.

6. Crèise, Stob a' Ghlais Choire and Sròn na Crèise.

47

The best route of ascent is by the north ridge, approximately the right-hand skyline as seen from the Hotel. There are several rock-steps on the ridge, but these are avoidable on the right and no difficulty will be found in reaching the Sròn and the easy ridge beyond to Stob a' Ghlais Choire.

The steep easterly face between the Stob and the Sròn affords a certain amount of climbing. The two prominent gullies on it were both climbed in July 1907 (J. Martin): that to the left branches half-way up and has one good pitch about 100 ft. above the left fork; that to the right is in two portions which join to form a deep-cut straight-edged gully, quite easy and of most interest near the top. The buttress to the left of the gullies was climbed in June 1903 (Dr. and Mrs. Inglis Clark) and gave a fairly continuous route on easy rocks. The buttress between them has also been climbed, about 1898 (J. S. Napier), but details are lacking.

There are in addition some rocks in the corrie to the south-east of the Stob. These are about 250 ft. high, fairly steep but loose. A route has been made up them direct to the summit, the climbing being reported of good standard all the way (D. W. Piggott).

Beinn Mhic Chasgaig (2820 ft.) – Four miles down Glen Etive, the west ridge of this peak terminates in a rounded granite buttress, Bird's Eye Buttress, well seen from the road near Dalness. Two routes on this crag are:

Surprise Pea. 300 ft. Very severe. (A. W. Ewing and A. McKeith. October 1966.) The start is at the foot of the buttress up a rib between two prominent corners. Trending leftwards, a jamming crack leads to a peg belay below a bulging slab, climbed to a perched block and final rib.

Fish Finger. 250 ft. Very severe. (A. McKeith and A. W. Ewing. October 1966.) Start 30 ft. up right from the lowest rocks (cairn) and climb a wall to a grass ledge and peg belay. A move to a prominent corner on the nose of the buttress leads to two sections of slab-climbing.

Secretion Slab. 400 ft. Severe. (A. McKeith. October 1966.) A steep narrow slab below and to the left of Bird's Eye Buttress.

7. Glen Etive from Beinn Trilleachan. In the centre the two Buachailles of Etive; to the right Stob Dubh, Beinn Ceitlein.

Two routes on A'Chioch, the afforested crag opposite the Dalness Chasm on Stob na Bròige, have also been recorded:

Weevil's Way. 300 ft. Severe. (J. Stenhouse and R. Marshall. July 1960.) Starts on the slabs at the left end of the crag and trends right.

Bo Weevil. 130 ft. Very severe. (D. Haston, J. Moriarty and G. B. Wakefield. Date uncertain.) Up the steep wall on the left of the crag.

Still farther on is the shapely western top of **Beinn Ceitlein, Stob Dubh** (2897 ft.), featuring prominently in views of the glen as one sails up to the head of Loch Etive. The glen itself, although ending in rather desolate flats, has scenery higher up which makes it one of the finest in Argyll. With its many falls and deep, shaded pools, the river is always worth exploring and there are innumerable camp-sites to be discovered beside it in the 9 miles of its course between Coupall Bridge and Coileitir.

It is said that the beautiful Deirdre had her *grianan* or sunny bower on one of the grassy slopes of Beinn Ceitlein across the river from Dalness. Here she roamed the hills with her lover Naoise, hunting the red deer and catching the salmon, happy in the short time they were to have together before they were persuaded to sail away with Fergus, Knight of the Red Branch, to final tragedy in Ireland.

BIBLIOGRAPHY

Always a Little Further. Alastair Borthwick. (John Smith, Glasgow. 1969.) (Upper Couloir of Stob Ghabhar.)
Scottish Mountains on Ski. Malcolm Slesser. (West Col.)
Tour in Scotland. Dorothy Wordsworth. (1803.)
Ski-ing in Scotland. Scottish Ski Club.

5

Glen Creran Hills

(1)   **Creach Bheinn** (2657 ft.). 3¾ miles E.S.E. of Creagan Station.
(2)   ***Beinn Sgulaird** (3059 ft.). 3 miles east of the head of Loch Creran.
(3)   **Beinn Trilleachan** (2752 ft.). 1½ miles W.S.W. of Kinlochetive pier.
(4)   ***Beinn Fhionnlaidh** (3139 ft.). 1½ miles south-west of (5).
(5)   ***Sgòr na h-Ulaidh** (3258 ft.). 3½ miles south of Clachaig Hotel, Glencoe.
(6)   **Stob an Fhuarain** (3160 ft.). ½ mile north-east of (5).

From the head of Loch Creran a pleasantly sheltered road leads up the glen past attractive out-of-the-world cottage clusters and with glimpses on the right of the river and Loch Baile Mhic Chailein. One can take a car up this road for 2½ miles to Elleric, just beyond the extensive oak wood of Coille Mheadhonach, an interesting type of Highland woodland that is in danger of disappearance and is attracting on that account the close attention of the Nature Conservancy. To begin with the glen itself is hemmed in closely on the left by steep, wooded slopes, but higher it offers a number of intriguing alternatives to the walker – westwards into Glen Duror, eastwards by way of Glen Ure to the head of Loch Etive, straight ahead to Loch Leven and Glencoe.

The hills described in this section lie to the east of Glen Creran and to the west of upper Loch Etive where the latter narrows to its head and merges into the river-flats beyond. To the north the boundary is Glencoe.

The twin-topped summit ridge of **Creach Bheinn** (2657 ft.) lies well back from Loch Creran and is defended low down along the loch-side by extensive afforestation. The easiest approach is from the north by way of the Allt Buidhe, thus avoiding the woods and allowing access to the north-east top (2636 ft.) over the shoulder named Meall Garbh on the one-inch map.

Beinn Sgulaird (3059 ft.) is a more impressive-looking hill, well seen from Glen Creran. Its switchback crest of fully 2 miles forms roughly the shape of an S running north-east and south-west. At the southern end of this ridge is a nameless top (2807 ft.), then a dip to 2597 ft., rise to Meall Garbh (2668 ft.), dip to 2579 ft., then the summit itself (3059 ft.). At yet another top (2963 ft.), $\frac{1}{5}$ mile farther on, the ridge divides: a spur runs east, dropping steeply enough to make scrambling necessary, while the main ridge continues easily round east-facing Coire nan Tulach to a saddle at 2087 ft. and finally Stob Gaibhre (2244 ft.)

The usual route of ascent is from the head of Loch Creran up the ridge which runs conveniently westwards from the southern top (2807 ft.). Thereafter, if the summit is traversed to Stob Gaibhre, a descent may be made easily into Glen Ure and the round completed with a walk down Glen Creran.

Beinn Sgulaird may also be climbed from Loch Etive head by the Allt a' Bhiorain, which passes round the north end of Beinn Trilleachan and leads to the headwaters of the Ure. From here the route lies up Stob Gaibhre and along the ridge to the summit.

From Glen Creran a pleasant route runs through the hills to Ballachulish village. There is a Forestry Commission road almost to the watershed, but permission to use this is advisable, especially as there is a gate on it liable to be padlocked. However, if one's car is left at Elleric, the walk through is only 7 miles and the saddle 1300 ft. It is worth noting that the two reservoirs connected by the Allt Eilidh are no longer filled full, their containing dams having been swept away in recent heavy flooding. Much of the area round the upper waters of the River Creran has been planted by the Forestry Commission, so that the alternative route through the hills, to Clachaig, while still possible, is not recommended.

The nearest way from Clachaig to Glen Etive is via Fionn Ghleann to its head over the Bealach Fhionnghaill (1914 ft.) and down by the Allt Charnan – a burn noteworthy for its magnificent rock-pools – to Invercharnan, $2\frac{1}{2}$ miles below Dalness.

Beinn Trilleachan (2752 ft.) – Seen to fine advantage as one sails up Loch Etive to its head, Beinn Trilleachan forms with Ben Starav an impressive gateway to the glen beyond. It is, however, on account of its magnificent sweep of granite slabs – the Etive Slabs – set comparatively low on the south face, that Beinn Trilleachan is now justly celebrated. The first climb, *Sickle*, was made in June 1954 by

8. The Glen Creran Hills from Beinn a' Bheithir. Sgòr na h-Ulaidh, the Bealach Caol Creran and the ridge of Beinn Fhionnlaidh.

E. D. G. Langmuir, J. A. Mallinson, M. J. O'Hara and Miss J. M. Tester, and so popular did the area become that by the summer of 1969 the total number of routes had been pushed up to 26.

Although the slabs are easy of access from the head of Loch Etive, it should be stressed that some of the routes are long and sustained, only one is graded less than very severe – and it is still severe – and everywhere a good technique in both free and artificial climbing is demanded; it is, as one writer has put it, 'as unique as gritstone climbing in England or hard ice-climbing in Scotland'.

The Long Walk, 1400 feet, climbed in May 1958 by J. Cunningham and M. Noon, is the longest route on the face apart from the *Girdle Traverse*, which was worked out over a period of some two years and completed in 1966 by B. Robertson and P. Nunn – a sustained very severe with one artificial A2 pitch midway.

53

Probably the most popular route is *Spartan Slab*, 575 ft. and again very severe, climbed in June 1954 by three of the pioneering party, E. D. G. Langmuir, M. J. O'Hara and J. A. Mallinson. The start is 10 ft. left of the huge flat-topped block lying below the Great Slab, almost centrally beneath the bow-shaped overhang and there are 6 pitches of exposed slab and crack climbing.

Variations on the same theme may be enjoyed on *Swastika*, another excellent very severe route of 685 ft. worked out by M. Noon and E. Taylor in June 1957. The start is 30 ft. past the tree to the left of Spartan Slab. However, to enjoy this splendid area to the full reference should be made to the guide book (S.M.C. *Climbers' Guide to Glencoe & Ardgour, Vol.* 2).

Beinn Fhionnlaidh (3139 ft.) has a rock-strewn plateau ⅜ mile long for a summit, with some interesting alpine flora, the highest point being the east end where there is a small cairn. East of the summit for a few yards the ridge is narrow and then there is a sudden drop with two steps, each of some 15 ft. and easily turned. The ridge then broadens out again and ½ mile from the summit a wire fence is struck, which ¼ mile farther on, just after passing over a small top (2694 ft.), turns north and the ridge descends steeply to the Bealach Caol Creran (1500 ft.), a descent of 1200 ft. in just over ½ mile. Every now and then the fence comes to an end on a perpendicular bluff and, even with good route-finding, some steep scrambling is called for. Under winter conditions, of course, special care is advisable. North-west from the summit plateau a small headland named Caoran (2944 ft.) juts out. On the north side of the summit plateau crags run down into Coire a' Chait, but no definite climb is likely to be found among them; on the south side, where the crags are more shattered and broken round Coireachan Odhar, some interesting scrambling may be had.

These crags may be included – to lend much or little variety to taste – on the best route of ascent. This is from Glenure Farm and along the north bank of the Allt Bealach na h-Innsig to Lochan na h-Uraich at 1000 ft.; continue for another ½ mile, then make uphill to the crags. Above them the plateau is reached not far from the summit. A more obvious, but less attractive route is by way of Glenure Farm and the long shoulder running out west from the summit to Leac Bharainn.

Sgòr na h-Ulaidh (3258 ft.) is the highest point of a broad ridge 2 miles long. From the summit the ridge goes north-east to **Stob an Fhuarain** (3160 ft.), then it turns north and is known as Aonach Dubh a' Ghlinne. West from the summit the ridge also continues briefly to a shoulder, Còrr na Beinne (2982 ft.). On the north side of the Sgòr is a steep rocky corrie, Coire Dubh, pierced by a gully – Red Gully – well seen from the north.

The usual route of ascent is from the Glencoe road where it crosses the foot of Fionn Ghleann, thence following the side-road up the glen to the cottage of Gleann-leac-na-muidhe. The steep 2000 ft. may then be climbed to the ridge, which is followed over several small tops to Stob an Fhuarain, or, preferably, a diagonal route may be chosen to the col between Aonach Dubh a' Ghlinne and Stob an Fhuarain. The direction thereafter is south-west to the main top. In summer the ridge presents no difficulty; under winter conditions of hard snow it should be treated with respect. In descent, however, following it is preferable to trying to find a way off the ridge too soon after leaving the summit; in any event do not strike west till Stob an Fhuarain is passed, when ordinary grass slopes will be met with. Going north from the Stob a gentle descent is followed by two slight rises before the final descent is commenced.

From Glen Creran the approach-route lies past Salachail, then east up the Caol Creran to Còrr na Beinne. If coming north from Beinn Fhionnlaidh by the Bealach Caol Creran, two routes offer themselves: one to the left, north-west, up an easy ridge over Còrr na Beinne to the top; the other to the right, north-east, following a wire fence for about ½ mile to a subsidiary col, the Bealach Clach nam Meirleach (2150 ft.), where the fence takes a sharp turn north-west and leads up to within 100 yards of the summit. On the east side of the hill there is a certain amount of rock affording some scrambling.

Red Gully. 650 ft. Very difficult. (D. Scott, R. Anderson, G. Allison and J. G. Black. March 1948.) The gully referred to above as conspicuous on the north face of Sgòr na h-Ulaidh directly below the summit cairn. There are four pitches of clean, reddish rock, the third being very difficult.

In February 1950 the gully was climbed under good winter conditions (D. Scott, J. C. Henderson and R. Anderson), time taken being just over 6 hours. The main problems were a 30-ft.

pitch of ice, snow-ice and powder snow; the crux, with a 100-ft. run-out ending on insecure dry powder on frozen turf; rightward traverse to a rock-rib; strenuous, airy work leading to a remarkable corner, easier rocks and the final snow-slopes of the gully. Since then the third pitch has been climbed avoiding the traverse to the rock-rib – by the left-hand corner, then right into a recess and up a steep 7-ft. wall.

Subsidiary Scoop. 500 ft. G.II. (Mr. and Mrs. I. Clough. March 1966.) Immediately to the left of Red Gully and separated from it by a rocky rib. Taken direct it gave a steep snow climb with two short steps of ice.

Vixen Gully, an easier snow gully with one or two short pitches just west of the summit, was descended glissading in March 1948 (R. Anderson, J. G. Black and G. Allison). A vixen crossed the foot of the gully below the party, hence its name.

West Gully. 1000 ft. (J. G. Parish, D. H. Haworth and J. S. Berkeley. February 1948.) Still farther west another snow gully, almost above the Sgòr na h-Ulaidh-Creag Bhàn col – a good steep climb, the finish being 30 ft. of difficult iced rock.

Humpback Gully. 1000 ft. G.II. (J. Renny, I. MacEacheran, R. Sharp and W. Sproul. November 1965.) On the north-east face of Creag Bhàn itself, the obvious gully to the right of the summit.

BIBLIOGRAPHY

Climbers' Guide to Glencoe and Ardgour. Volume 2. L. S. Lovat. (S.M.C. 1965.) (Beinn Trilleachan).

9. *Opposite :* Glencoe: Aonach Dubh a' Ghlinne from near Clachaig.

6

Glencoe – South side

(1) *Buachaille Etive Mòr – Stob Dearg (3345 ft.). $2\frac{1}{4}$ miles west of Kingshouse Hotel.

(2) Stob na Doire (3250 ft.). $1\frac{1}{4}$ miles south-west of (1).

(3) Stob Coire Altruim (3065 ft.). $\frac{5}{8}$ mile W.S.W. of (2).

(4) Stob na Bròige (3120 ft.). $\frac{1}{2}$ mile south-west of (3).

(5) *Buachaille Etive Beag – Stob Dubh (3130 ft.). 1 mile north-west of (4).

(6) Stob Coire Raineach (3029 ft.). $1\frac{1}{4}$ miles north-east of (5).

(7) *Bidean nam Bian (3766 ft.). $1\frac{3}{4}$ miles S.E. by S. of Clachaig Inn.

(8) Stob Coire nam Beith (3621 ft.). $\frac{1}{3}$ mile north-west of (7).

(9) Stob Coire nan Lochan (3657 ft.). $\frac{1}{2}$ mile N.N.E. of (7).

(10) Stob Coire Sgreamhach (3497 ft.). $\frac{3}{4}$ mile E.S.E. of (7).

(11) Beinn Fhada (3120 ft.). $\frac{1}{2}$ mile north-east of (10).

(12) Beinn Fhada, North-East Top (3064 ft.). $\frac{3}{4}$ mile north-east of (10).

(13) Beinn Maol Chaluim (2967 ft.). $1\frac{3}{4}$ miles north-west of Inbhirfhaolain, Glen Etive.

'He who has time must be told that all the beauty of Glenco will not be found from the road side.'

So wrote the discerning Dr. John Macculloch as long ago as 1824, and few who are in any way familiar with the variety of rock and ridge and corrie would argue that his words are any less apt today.

Glencoe is probably the most widely known and celebrated of all the Scottish glens, not only historically but on account of the scale and impressiveness of its wild, austere scenery. From its head just west of the great rock-cathedral of Buachaille Etive Mòr down to the woods and pasture-lands that reach the last $2\frac{1}{2}$ miles from Clachaig to the shore of Loch Leven interest never lessens: on the one hand the dark successive threats of the 'Three Sisters' – Beinn Fhada, Geàrr Aonach and Aonach Dubh – on the other the long, steep wall that climbs to the jagged skyline saw-edge of the Aonach Eagach. Characteristically, high corries – impossible to see in detail from the road – reach back into the recesses of Bidean nam Bian, while the gullies which score and seam the rock-faces hold turbulent burns in their depths, falling to the gorge of the Coe and, lower down, to the bleak, wind-scoured waters of Loch Achtriochtan.

58

Appropriately the story of the glen goes far back into the mists at the beginnings of history, when Fingal or Fionn and the giants who were his followers, lived and fought and hunted there. Still commemorating those far-off days are, for example, Sgòr nam Fiannaidh, 'peak of the Fingalians', and Ossian's Cave above Loch Achtriochtan, named after the celebrated poet son of Fingal.

The glen itself belonged in early clan days first to the Macdougalls, then from the time of Robert the Bruce to the Macdonalds. In due time, however, the power of Clan Donald began to decline and the

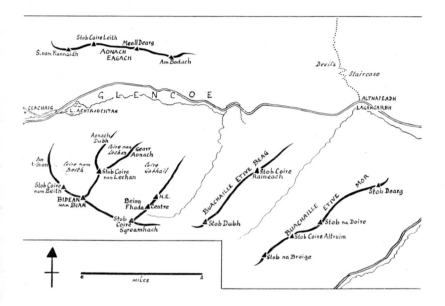

Glencoe lands were granted by the Crown to the Stewarts of Appin, who thus became the feudal superiors of the Macdonalds. But the power of the Campbells was in the ascendant and later in the sixteenth century it was the Earls of Argyll who, in turn, became superiors to the Stewarts. No love was lost between Macdonalds and Campbells, and many and bitter were the forays which the former carried out, bringing back the fat Campbell cattle to the secure fastnesses of Glencoe.

In 1644 the Macdonalds of Glencoe followed Montrose during his whirlwind campaign of the Civil War, which took them plundering right through Campbell country. Then, in 1688, they fought

59

10. Buachaille Etive Mòr, Stob Dearg – Winter.

with Bonnie Dundee at Killiecrankie, returning home through Campbell of Glenlyon's land, which they plundered ruthlessly, leaving Glenlyon a ruined man.

After the Killiecrankie campaign, William III decreed that all rebellious Highland chiefs were to take an Oath of Allegiance to the Crown before January 1, 1692. For various reasons MacIan, the old chief of the Macdonalds of Glencoe, put off this duty. When finally he presented himself before Colonel Hill at Fort William on December 31, he found that he must travel to Inveraray to take the oath. Delayed by blizzards, he eventually arrived there on January 2 and on the 6th the oath was duly administered, MacIan thereafter returning confidently home.

However, the Master of Stair, Secretary of State to William, was determined to make an example of the Macdonalds and forwarded the order from the King 'to extirpate that sept of thieves'; later instructions from him urged that 'it be secret and sudden'.

On February 1 a company of 120 men of Argyll's regiment under the command of Captain Robert Campbell of Glenlyon, victim of the Macdonalds' raid after Killiecrankie, appeared in the glen and billeted themselves in the various Macdonald houses. There were three or five to a cottage, from Carnoch eastward to Achtriochtan, and with Glenlyon himself at Inverrigan. For two weeks the troops enjoyed the hospitality of the Macdonalds, living with them on the best of terms.

On February 12 800 soldiers under Major Duncanson left Fort William to co-operate with Glenlyon in carrying out the Master of Stair's orders and to ensure that the escape routes via Kinlochleven and the upper part of Glencoe were sealed. A message was sent on ahead to Glenlyon ordering him to 'putt all to the sword under 70'.

Before first light on February 13 the massacre began: shots were heard at Inverrigan and Achnacon and the old chief was shot from behind in his own house. Tradition has it that it was at his summer house of Gleann-leac-na-muidhe that MacIan died, and indeed uneasiness may have prompted him to move there even although in the month of February it would have had fewer comforts than his main residence of Invercoe. About 38 defenceless men, women and children were killed, but those who fled from their blazing homes had to face blizzard and storm in the high passes of the hills and many must have died of exposure and starvation. Some of the survivors climbed over the western shoulder of Meall Mòr or round its eastern flank past Gleann-leac-na-muidhe; others would have to choose the opposite direction, through the snow of the Lairig Gartain or up into the doubtful sanctuary of Coire Gabhail.

The whole ghastly story raised a bitter outcry at the time – 'This business of Glencoe makes a scurvy noise' – but significantly no real attempt was made to punish the ringleaders.

Despite the losses suffered in the massacre and later, on the Jacobite side, in the risings of 1715 and 1745, the population of the glen actually appears to have increased; indeed by the end of the eighteenth century there are suggestions of over-population. Numerically, the coming of sheep had more serious effects and by 1803 Dorothy Wordsworth was to be told by her Highland driver 'that formerly the glen had had many inhabitants, and that there, as elsewhere in the

Highlands, there had been a great deal of corn where now the lands were left waste'. Following the Wordsworths and Coleridge, many other famous travellers were to pass through the glen – Southey, for one, along with Telford in 1819, Dickens in 1841, Queen Victoria in 1873. An inn had been opened at Clachaig by 1839 and here, from 1843 onwards, the celebrated stage-coach 'Marquis of Breadalbane' would halt on its long-distance runs between Inverness and Glasgow. In 1933, despite a storm of protest which had been rumbling for years, the present road through the glen was opened, replacing the switchback of grassy corners and hump-backed bridges which had served for so long.

In 1935 and 1937 the finest part of the area was acquired by the National Trust for Scotland – in great measure through the financial help given by the S.M.C., the various other mountaineering clubs and the Pilgrim Trust – to be held in perpetuity for the nation. The actual boundaries of this property of 12,800 acres are: from Altnafeadh to Dalness round Buachaille Etive Mòr following the course of the Coupall and the Etive; from Dalness over the main ridge of Bidean nam Bian to Achnacon and Clachaig; thence along the Aonach Eagach to Am Bodach, down to the glen again and so back to Altnafeadh. The actual scene of the massacre is not part of the property, but the acquisition of the rest of the glen by the Trust will save it from possible exploitation. Free and unrestricted access to all the mountains, corries and glens is permitted at all times. An information centre is open at the large lay-by on the main road, A82, opposite Clachaig (G.R. NN 125564).

Buachaille Etive Mòr, Stob Dearg (3345 ft.) – Lying in the angle between Glencoe and Glen Etive, 'The Buachaille' as it is popularly called presents its boldest face, Stob Dearg, towards Kingshouse and Rannoch Moor. Rising direct from the moor without the distraction of intervening minor heights, its cone of dark, shattered rock makes it in every way one of the finest mountains in Scotland. Summer or winter, as one travels north-west into the throat of Glencoe, one's gaze is drawn repeatedly upwards by the complex sequence of buttress and gully.

Rock, snow and ice routes of every grade of difficulty are to be had on the north and east faces of Stob Dearg, the rock being a

11. Buachaille Etive Mòr, Stob Dearg – Summer.

coarse and reliable rhyolite. One of the earliest routes in Scottish rock-climbing history was made on it, by Professor Norman Collie, G. A. Solly and J. Collier, from a camp at the foot of 'The Buachaille', in March, 1894; today the popularity of the face leaves no doubt that it has the best rock-climbing in Glencoe to offer.

Stob Dearg may be ascended without serious climbing either from the north or from the south. From the S.M.C's Lagangarbh Hut, 3 miles west of Kingshouse, a way should be made up into the corrie directly above – Coire na Tulaich – which is flanked on the east by Stob Dearg and lower, on the west, by Stob Coire nan Tuileachan.

63

12. The Dalness Chasm on Stob na Bròige, Buachaille Etive Mòr.

From here the summit ridge is gained at the col (2900 ft.) some 600 yards west of the cairn, after a rough scramble over screes. Thereafter the walk to the top is equally straightforward. The col may also be reached from 2½ miles down the Glen Etive road by way of the steep grassy slopes of Coire Cloiche Finne.

To reach the col in descent from the summit, proceed 300 yards W.S.W. (magnetic), then 300 yards due west. Thereafter turn north or south to choice. These are the most convenient ways off the mountain in winter, particularly for those who do not know it well.

Although Stob Dearg is the highest top, the mountain itself stretches back W.S.W. and parallel to Glen Etive for another 3 miles. **Stob na Doire** (3250 ft.), not named on the 1-inch O.S. map, lies 1¼ miles south-west of Stob Dearg round the grassy Coire Cloiche Finne. From the lowest points of the connecting ridge (2900 ft.) the Bidean nam Bian group shows up well in outline. Next on the ridge, **Stob Coire Altruim** (3065 ft.) – a local name not found on the maps – is reached after a drop to 2600 ft. The rocks of its bold summit appear inviting as seen from the Glencoe road, but the climbing is disappointing and its potentialities are negligible. *Centre Gully*, on this north face, gave a winter climb of about 300 ft., with two short pitches of snow-ice, in February, 1950 (T. Graham Brown and J. G. Parish). The further ½ mile to the final top, **Stob na Bròige** (3120 ft.), barely falls below the 3000-ft. contour. On it, facing Alltchaoruinn 4 miles down the Glen Etive road, is the formidable 1200-ft. gully system of the *Dalness Chasm*. The latter was first climbed, by its severe left-hand fork, in June 1951 (J. Cunningham and H. MacInnes; S. Jagger and C. White), while the very severe central fork was done four years later (J. R. Marshall, A. H. Hendry and D. Boston; L. S. Lovat and T. Weir). The right prong has not so far been climbed. From the summit of Stob na Bròige a splendid view down Loch Etive is to be had, while in the reverse direction, looking towards the peak from the loch and lower reaches of the glen, it and Stob Dubh of Buachaille Etive Beag present two beautifully symmetrical cones connected by the deep bealach of the Lairig Gartain (1600 ft.).

Apart from the areas mentioned, any of these subsidiary tops may be ascended almost anywhere without serious climbing. About 1½ hours will be found easy time from Stob Dearg to Stob na Bròige, while if the day's expedition be continued to include Buachaille

Etive Beag, another $1\frac{1}{2}$ hours may be reckoned for the drop to the Lairig Gartain and re-ascent to Stob Dubh.

Excluding variations, the number of climbing-routes on the Buachaille now totals approximately 150. In the summary which follows an attempt has been made to pay regard to the makings of history, as well as to variety of gradings, so that unavoidably a great many modern routes of high standard have had to be passed over. Full details, however, are to be found in the S.M.C. *Climbers' Guide to Glencoe*. Volume 1 (Buachaille Etive Mòr), while climbs pioneered after 1959 are on record in the S.M.C. *Journal*. The routes are here described, as in the rock-guide, from north-west to south-east.

On the lowest slopes of Stob Coire nan Tuileachan, above Lagangarbh, the face of Creag a' Bhancair has provided a distinctive and very steep route of 655 feet – *Carnivore* (J. Cunningham and M. Noon. August 1958) – its exposed cracks and long traverses, with numerous piton belays, typifying much recent achievement of very severe standard. Elsewhere in Coire na Tulaich a dozen or so lesser routes varying in length from 100 to 300 ft. and in grading from moderate to very severe, are equally accessible and offer some worthwhile sport for an evening or a short day.

The North Face section of Buachaille, which includes the cliffs between Coire na Tulaich and North Buttress, was remarkably late in being opened up. Discounting the 1200 ft. of *Great Gully*, where Professor Norman Collie in 1894 was the first to sample its 'wet rock garnished with watercresses and other aquatic plants', it was not until 1930 that the relatively short *Lagangarbh Chimney* and the much more important *Cuneiform Buttress (Ordinary Route)* were discovered. The latter, pioneered by J. H. B. Bell and A. Harrison, became a particularly popular 'very difficult' in the thirties. Among more recent climbs on the Cuneiform are three on the west face, the first of these, *Snowba's*, 400 ft. and very severe, having been done in May 1968 by C. Higgins and J. McLean. Dividing the Cuneiform from North Buttress is the dark, vertical slit of *Raven's Gully*, an 11-pitch climb of real character. The first party, in June 1937, consisted of J. B. Nimlin, B. Braithwaite, N. Millar, J. Macfarlane and A. N. Other, and their grading of very severe still stands. A direct finish was added in 1948 and the winter ascent of the ordinary route, for which favourable conditions are essential, was done in February 1953 (H. MacInnes and C. Bonington).

Since the war there has been a spate of climbing on this section of

13. Crowberry Gully, Buachaille Etive Mòr.

the Buachaille, in particular on Slime Wall, the exposed West Face of
North Buttress. Two short 160 ft. routes, *Belial* and *Pluto*, had
been made here in 1940, but it was not until June 1948 that the first
of the 'very severes', *Guerdon Grooves*, was worked out by J. Cunningham and W. Smith, in its day the hardest climb in Glencoe. *Bludger's*

67

Route in September 1952 and *Revelation* in June 1956 were to follow, both led by P. Walsh, but it was not until June 1958 that the length of Guerdon Grooves was fractionally outstripped by the 550 ft. of *Shibboleth* (R. Smith and A. Frazer), a fine climb taking the most direct line up the whole cliff. Also of 550 ft., *Apocalypse* was added by C. Higgins and I. Nicolson in June 1969.

The second major division which has been made for descriptive purposes – the North-East Face – comprises four buttresses and three gullies. As viewed from the Glencoe road, these are from right to left: North Buttress, Crowberry Gully, Crowberry Ridge, Easy Gully, Curved Ridge, D Gully and D Gully Buttress. Here, in earlier days, the major part of the mountain's climbing history was made and here today the classic routes still attract a popularity which is certainly not lessening.

Inevitably the 1000-ft. *North Buttress* drew the attention of the early pioneers and in July 1895 it was climbed by W. Brown, Rose and W. Tough. In summer, with careful route-selection, this broad buttress gives a thoroughly enjoyable 'moderate' allowing considerable variation; under snow and ice conditions the problems can be very different, with verglas in cracks and chimneys consuming valuable time before the easier-angled upper slopes can be gained.

On the interesting East Face of North Buttress there are a number of routes, mostly severe or very severe and mostly comparatively short. Longer than the majority, at 300 ft., a *Girdle Traverse* was worked out by J. R. Jackson and K. Robson in September 1967.

Crowberry Gully, the deep-cut 1000-ft. gully which separates North Buttress from Crowberry Ridge, owes a well-deserved reputation to its winter rather than its summer merits. Since its first winter ascent in February 1936 by W. M. Mackenzie, J. B. Russell, J. F. Hamilton and J. K. W. Dunn, it has come to be recognised, on account of its beauty and character as much as for its length, as one of the great Scottish classics. Six to ten hours are reckoned as normal time for the climb, which usually finishes by way of the right fork. Parallel to the gully and running up the northern wall of Crowberry Ridge, the *Shelf Route* presents another, harder winter climb. First ascended by W. H. Murray and W. M. Mackenzie, leading through, in March 1937, it was one of the epic winter climbs which these two mountaineers pioneered at that period of breakaway from tradition and new discovery.

Directly under the summit and curving upwards to its unmistakable

Tower, *Crowberry Ridge* is probably the most celebrated climb on the Buachaille. Originally ascended in August 1896 by W. W. Naismith and W. Douglas, this line was bettered in May 1900 by G. D. Abraham, A. P. Abraham, J. W. Puttrell and E. A. Baker, who took the Direct Route by the famous left traverse from Abraham's Ledge. Forming its east and south-east face is the well-known Rannoch Wall, with a network of more than a dozen interesting and exposed routes. The Wall attracted particularly keen attention in the early thirties, *Route I* falling eventually to G. C. Williams, G. F. Todd, G. Graham Macphee and I. G. Jack in June 1934. Two years later the longer and much more satisfying line of *Agag's Groove* was taken by J. F. Hamilton, A. Anderson and A. C. D. Small; today, as the most popular route on the mountain, this climb is not unusually readily identifiable by the length of the queue at its foot. The Groove, 350 ft. overall, emerges on the crest of Crowberry Ridge above the latter's slabs and is rated as a 'very difficult'. Among later discoveries on the Wall, *January Jigsaw* – one of three routes made by H. I. Ogilvy and Miss E. Speakman – is comparable in standard to Agag's Groove; *Whortleberry Wall*, a line of 390 ft. followed by J. Cunningham and W. Smith, is the longest of several 'very severes'.

Bending round the Rannoch Wall and forming an excellent grandstand for the climbing there is *Curved Ridge*, the easiest rock-route on Buachaille and in summer a time-honoured, enjoyable way of descent. It begins at a height of 2100 ft. and ends a short distance below the base of Crowberry Tower. To reach it returning from the summit, descend due east to the Crowberry Tower Gap, skirt the Tower by an easy gully on its right and go left at the base to the top of the ridge.

Beyond Curved Ridge, *D Gully Buttress* – noteworthy for its very difficult 60-ft. slab crux – merges at its top with the crest of the considerably more spacious *Central Buttress*. The latter has provided much excellent climbing since the original pioneering was done in 1898. Several routes are to the credit of Dr. J. H. B. Bell, notably the major portion of *North Face*, which he and A. Harrison discovered in July 1929 and which is described as offering 'a great variety of climbing by walls, cracks, corners, chimneys, slabs and traverses.' On a 7-hour winter ascent in January 1958 – by R. Marshall and J. Stenhouse – difficulties, some very severe, were encountered on every pitch.

Even with the tally of routes and variations on Central Buttress

mounting to well over a dozen, it was still possible for two 'very severes' to be recorded comparatively recently: *Rock Climb* by J. Knight and A. McKeith in April 1965 and *Apauling* by A. McKeith and P. Brian in May 1966.

From Central Buttress, the third and final section of climbs – the South-East Face – continues past *Collie's Climb*, the first rock-route ever made on the mountain, to *The Chasm*, a magnificent gully cutting deeply into the mountainside for 1420 ft. Climbing starts about 20 minutes' walk from the Glen Etive road, and interest, like the rock scenery, improves the higher one progresses up the 16 pitches. The final problem, escape from the Devil's Cauldron, offers three possibilities, of which the Direct Route – wet, 130 ft., and very severe – was climbed in August 1931 by I. G. Jack and J. G. Robinson.

Beyond The Chasm – apart from *South Gully*, which is of only minor importance – there is no further climbing.

Buachaille Etive Beag, Stob Dubh (3130 ft.) – Although bearing a striking resemblance to its bigger neighbour, the 'Little Buachaille' is a mountain of very much less character. Its familiar north-eastern nose, Stob nan Cabar (2547 ft.), outthrust like Stob Dearg over the entrance to Glencoe, is steep, but without the interest of any continuous rock. Its flanks consist for the most part of grass and high-angle scree, tedious in summer and demanding considerable respect under snow and ice. The main peak, Stob Dubh, lies at the south-western end of the summit ridge, 150 yards N.N.E. of the point marked 3129 ft. on the 1-inch O.S. map. From it slopes fall steeply west to the Lairig Eilde (1600 ft.) and equally steeply E.S.E. to the Lairig Gartain (1600 ft.), the two low passes through to Dalness, in Glen Etive. The subsidiary top, **Stob Coire Raineach** (3029 ft.), lies just over 1 mile north-east of the summit after a drop to 2450 ft. The southern flank of the ridge between Stob Coire Raineach and Stob nan Cabar is seamed by four gullies, of which the second from the right, No. 3 – named *Red Campion Gully* – gave a difficult climb of about 1000 ft. in June 1950 (J. G. Parish, T. Graham Brown, E. W. Scott and G. S. Boon). The left fork of the gully was followed. The two gullies to the left were found to be disappointing; that to the right has apparently not been explored.

14. *Opposite:* Rannoch Moor and Schichallion from the summit of Buachaille Etive Mòr.

Bidean nam Bian (3766 ft.) – As befits the highest mountain in Argyll, Bidean nam Bian possesses outstanding interest and character. It was first climbed, in the cause of botany, as early as 1772; on the North Face of Aonach Dubh the local shepherd Neil Marquis is reputed to have reached Ossian's Cave in 1868, the first recorded rock-climb in Glencoe; today the mountain's popularity is never in question.

Unfortunately, although Bidean nam Bian is one of the finest mountain groups in Scotland, its tops are so steep and closely clustered that it is impossible to get a satisfactory overall view of them except from high on some more or less distant peak – from the Mamores, for instance, where Bidean is the dominating feature of the views and not even the Ben Nevis group rivals it in majesty and beauty of outline. The actual summit of Bidean itself is so shut off by its outliers that only a glimpse of it is to be had – behind the two great rock buttresses, the Diamond and the Church Door – from the floor of Glencoe, near Clachaig Inn. On the other hand, what can be seen is altogether satisfying: deep, tree-hidden gorges leading up between the steep north-facing spurs to Coire Gabhail, Coire nan Lochan and Coire nam Beith, with, higher still, an occasional glimpse of the ridge-crest linking the sharp tops of Beinn Fhada, ice-fluted cliffs on Stob Coire nan Lochan, or the extensive West Face of Aonach Dubh, its buttresses catching perhaps the glow of a fiery sunset.

Bidean nam Bian is usually climbed by way of Coire nam Beith. From the bridge across the Coe at the west end of Loch Achtriochtan, the true left bank of the burn dropping from the corrie is followed up steep grassy slopes and past several fine waterfalls. A path then leads through a narrow ravine to cross the stream ½ mile farther on at a point where two branches unite (1750 ft.). The left-hand branch is followed to the boulder field of the upper corrie, whence steep scree-slopes climb leftwards to the saddle between Bidean and **Stob Coire nan Lochan** (3657 ft.). The ridge from this saddle to the summit is narrow and fairly steep, but except under severe winter conditions is just a walk; in descent care should be taken lest one of the short ridges running out left to either of the twin buttresses near the summit be followed by mistake. From the saddle to the top of Stob Coire nan Lochan the stretch of ridge is broader and easier than that to the main summit.

Other routes to Bidean from the upper corrie may be taken by breaking out right instead of left, to the saddles west or east of **Stob Coire nam Beith** (3621 ft.), or up the scree-slopes beside the Church Door Buttress, the right-hand of the two great buttresses ahead, to the dip in the ridge immediately west of the summit.

Yet another alternative is to reach this north-west ridge by way of

15. Avalanche debris (March), Coire nam Beith.

An t-Sròn (2750 ft.) – easily climbed from the stream-fork at 1750 ft., or else straight up the steep face from the main road opposite Clachaig. This latter choice means avoiding the deep gash of the prominent An t-Sròn Chasm and involves a tiresome stretch of large scree higher up, but it is rewarded with an interesting ridge-walk over

73

Stob Coire nam Beith and the little intervening subsidiary top which follows.

The third ridge of Bidean descends first south-east then E.S.E. to reach **Stob Coire Sgreamhach** (3497 ft.) in about ¾ mile. It then swings north-east as the long shoulder of Beinn Fhada. The first ½ mile of this shoulder to the **Centre Top** of Beinn Fhada (3120 ft.), not marked on the 1-inch O.S. map, involves some scrambling on the descent of the last 100 ft. or so to the col, and care should be taken in mist; a short, steep gully slightly to the right offers an easier alternative to the actual face. Beyond the rocky Centre Top the ridge continues for ¼ mile over the **North-East Top** (3064 ft.) and drops in another ⅓ mile to a grassy saddle with two cairns. The ridge beyond this point leads to the precipitous nose of Beinn Fhada and should not be followed; instead one can descend steeply left into Coire Gabhail or almost as steeply right to the Lairig Eilde and the well-cairned path which leads back eventually to Glencoe near the Meeting of the Three Waters.

It was to Coire Gabhail – 'the corrie of capture, or booty', or, as it is now much more commonly called, 'the Lost Valley' – that the clansmen used to drive their cattle for safety and in it no doubt more often hid those that had been stolen. So steep are its sides, so level is its floor and so narrow its entrance that it must indeed have provided the perfect hideout. A visit to the Lost Valley is well worth while for its own sake and may be made without difficulty from the bridge over the Coe opposite Allt-na-Reigh cottage, ½ mile west of the Meeting of the Three Waters. From the bridge a muddy track leads up the true left bank of the Allt Coire Gabhail and through a deep gorge luxuriant with birches and rowans. The path then crosses to the right bank and climbs through a barrier of chaotic, tumbled rocks, beneath which the burn disappears, out to the floor of the corrie – a pleasant ½ mile stretch of shingle and grass. At the corrie-mouth a gigantic rock pyramid known as 'The Boulder' offers some enjoyable problem climbing with a variety of routes up to 25 ft. in length. On either side of the corrie the steep slopes of Geàrr Aonach and Beinn Fhada, and at its head the even higher containing ridge linking Bidean and Stob Coire Sgreamhach, give to the whole place a remarkable atmosphere of Himalayan seclusion and remoteness.

The smaller Coire nan Lochan, between Geàrr Aonach and Aonach Dubh, is also reached by a tree-fringed rock gorge and rises to a cluster of lochans at just over 2500 ft. under the very fine range of summit cliffs. From this north-eastern side Stob Coire nan Lochan itself may be reached by way of either of its outliers, Geàrr Aonach or Aonach Dubh, although approaching from the former, a cleft in the ridge some 400 ft. below the summit should be treated with respect.

Bidean nam Bian may also, as a variation, be climbed from Glen Etive by way of Gleann Fhaolain, although this route, lacking the interest of the northern approaches, is more commonly used on the descent – sometimes, it has been observed, in error. The Allt Fhaolain passes Inbhirfhaolain, the Grampian Club's hut, on its way down to the Etive, draining a deep horseshoe of hills, the south-western arm of which culminates in **Beinn Maol Chaluim** (2967 ft.). From this 'Corbett' the ridge runs northwards to a bealach at 2400 ft. before climbing again north-eastwards to the main summit of Bidean.

All the climbing on the Bidean nam Bian massif lies on the Glencoe flanks and is of remarkable variety and interest. Some of the routes – which now number well over 150 – are vegetatious and loose; others are on rock which allows full play for modern techniques and which has been yielding a great many discoveries of the highest standards.

With the exception of Neil Marquis's visit to Ossian's Cave a century ago, all the earliest climbing on Bidean was done around Coire nam Beith. In 1894 Professor Norman Collie worked his way out to the top of his *Pinnacle*, at the foot of the Central Gully between the Church Door and Diamond Buttresses. He and his party also explored the *Church Door Buttress* itself, but it was Harold Raeburn, J. H. Bell, H. C. Boyd and R. G. Napier who actually made history with this classic climb four years later, following what is now known as *Flake Route*. The seventy years since the first ascent of the buttress have confirmed its popularity and produced more than half a dozen new routes, notably on its west face. Across Central Gully, *Diamond Buttress* in summer is too vegetatious to offer serious competition, although in January 1959 it afforded J. McLean and M. Noon a 500-ft. Grade IV. *Bishop's Buttress*, just west of the Church Door, gave three new 'very severes' in summer 1968.

Around the turn of the century the attention of the explorers – who included the well-known Lakeland climber, G. D. Abraham – was attracted to an area of obvious possibilities, the complicated West Face of Aonach Dubh. A close look was also being taken at the impressive cone of Stob Coire nam Beith, the first actual climb there being recorded in 1900. Stob Coire nam Beith was much in favour

75

in the thirties, when Dr. Bell, C. M. Allan, and A. Harrison were among those particularly active on it, but it was not until 1946 that *The Sphinx*, 450 ft. in length, difficult, and the steepest buttress on the mountain was climbed by W. H. Murray and R. Smith; to this a severe direct variant was added in August 1967 by Mr. and Mrs. I. Clough and J. Simpson. Meanwhile, in April 1939, W. M. Mackenzie and W. H. Murray had highlighted the much greater, winter attractions of Stob Coire nam Beith by making a magnificent first ascent of *Deep-Cut Chimney*. The fashion had been set. Numerous other winter routes followed, for example the particularly rewarding severities of 600-ft. *Arch Gully*, while among the winter buttresses climbed, *The Sphinx*, in January 1958, gave J. R. Marshall and I. Douglas $3\frac{1}{2}$ hours of sustained difficulty.

On the West Face of Aonach Dubh, the complex triple-tiered rhyolite and andesite buttresses have offered great scope for summer exploration. Among the discoveries on this extensive face and in the high-level basin known as The Amphitheatre are four routes by Dr. J. H. B. Bell and C. M. Allan in the thirties and six by L. S. Lovat with various seconds in the fifties. The most difficult and most interesting area is, however, E Buttress, on which the number of 'very severes' has been mounting impressively since the summer of 1958, when J. R. Marshall led both the severe *Original Route* and the very severe *Trapeze*. In June 1959 *Hee-Haw* was climbed by J. Moriarty and D. Haston and this was followed by *The Big Top* by R. Smith and J. Gardener in August 1961. Still the buttress was not worked out, the summer of 1966 seeing yet more additions, including *Sideshow* by J. R. Marshall, while the traditional *Girdle Traverse* came in June 1967 from M. Galbraith and A. McKeith. In December 1965 the winter possibilities of the face were indicated when I. S. Clough and D. G. Roberts climbed the Grade III/IV *Christmas Couloir*. Then, in February and March 1969, no less than eight further winter routes, all Grade II and III, were pioneered, showing perhaps where future opportunities lie.

Returning to the farther, north end of the face, it should be noted that the fastest and easiest route down from the ridge, either winter or summer, starts at the col between Aonach Dubh and Stob Coire nan Lochan, following the easy upper part of No. 2 Gully and, when it steepens below Middle Ledge, traversing right on to Dinner-time Buttress. Alternatively the easy *Dinner-time Buttress* itself, with only some 150 ft. of rock high up, may be followed the whole way down.

The North Face of Aonach Dubh overlooking Glencoe is especially familiar on account of the deep black gash of Ossian's Cave. Below the latter a long waterfall gully inclines down to the right across the lower face and this may be easily followed upwards until a right traverse can be made without difficulty on to Sloping Shelf which climbs westwards to easy ground and is the easiest route up the cliffs. From the Shelf, directly below the cave, a difficult climb – *Ossian's Ladder* – leads up on unpleasant, vegetatious rock to the actual cave floor, which is tilted at an angle of 45°. A visitors' book in a metal box is kept at the back of the cave.

One of the earliest climbs on Bidean, *Shadbolt's Chimney*, made by A. C. McLaren and L. G. Shadbolt in June 1908, starts a few yards to the left of Ossian's Ladder and is still recognised as a route of character. Elsewhere the face is now crowded with more than a dozen 'very severes'. *Stook* and *Yo-Yo* in April and May 1959 were both led by R. Smith; the 500 ft. of *Tober* by I. S. Clough and D. G. Roberts six years later equalled in length the earlier *Fingal's Chimney*, by J. Brown and L. S. Lovat; also mainly a chimney climb, *Fall-out* was added to the growing list in May 1968 by J. Ferguson and C. Higgins.

On the East Face of Aonach Dubh probably the most interesting feature is the Main Crag, a range of rhyolite cliffs 400 yards long and 600 ft. high, situated about 1000 ft. above the Glencoe road. It is worth noting that there is an excellent bivouac site under an overhang on the east side of the glen facing the centre of this cliff. Here in May 1947, W. H. Murray, D. B. McIntyre and T. J. Ransley did no less than seven new climbs ranging in grade from moderate to very difficult, perhaps the most outstanding being *Archer Ridge*, 'a distinctive route on superb rock'. The discovery of a completely new range of climbs suitable for those of more modest ambitions was certainly an event of note. A recent very severe addition here has been the 600 ft. *Girdle Traverse of Terrace Face* in September 1969 by K. V. Crocket, D. C. Forest and D. M. Jenkins.

Below the summit of Stob Coire nan Lochan, the magnificently situated north-east corrie contains five buttresses and six gullies, the floor of the corrie lying at approximately 2700 ft. and the cliffs above rising to a height of some 500 ft. Excellent winter climbing of all grades of difficulty is to be had in the gullies, with, recently, one or two new buttress routes added; in summer the climbing is almost all on the buttresses, but is less satisfactory than might be expected. A good straightforward snow-climb, without any serious difficulty, is

77

N.C. Gully; *S.C. Gully* is a much more serious proposition, an attractive snow and ice climb first done in March 1934. More lately, in February 1956 on Summit Buttress, *Scabbard Chimney* gave L. S. Lovat, J. R. Marshall and A. H. Hendry an exacting climb of 5 hours – Lovat having already led the first summer ascent in 1954.

16. Beinn Fhada, Buachaille Etive Beag and Etive Mòr from Bidean nam Bian.

Also on this buttress are *Pearly Gates*, a 500-ft. Grade II done in April 1966, and *The Duel*, 300 ft. and very severe, in June 1967.

Two climbing areas of Bidean remain to be mentioned, both relatively new discoveries; these are Geàrr Aonach and Beinn Fhada. The North Face of the former, the middle of the Three Sisters, overlooks Glencoe with a forbidding steepness. At its eastern edge some enjoyable scrambling on good rock is to be had; centrally the climbing is much more serious, the best of some half-dozen routes probably being *The Kneepad*, a 550-ft. 'very severe' up a wall and steep cracks almost at the highest point of the face. This was first climbed in May 1959 by D. Haston, J. Moriarty and J. R. Marshall, being given a direct introduction two years later by Haston and Moriarty. On the East Face of Geàrr Aonach two sections of cliff, accessible from Coire Gabhail, have come into favour since 1952 and each now offers a choice of more than a dozen routes ranging from 150 to 450 ft. Also newly added, mainly in February 1969, nearly a dozen Grade II–IV routes up to 1000 ft. in length make the face an interesting new winter attraction.

Finally Beinn Fhada's east flank gives *Sròn na Lairig*, a 1000-ft. snow ridge, and a 270-ft. summer 'very difficult', *Kak.* At the head of Coire Gabhail the fare is better: both Lost Valley Buttress and Lost Valley Minor Buttress have provided some recent hard routes, summer and winter. Originally climbed by R. G. Donaldson and J. E. Spence in the summer of 1942, the former gave *Sabre Tooth*, a Grade III, in February 1969 and the Grade IV *Tyrannosaur* in March 1969. Longest on the minor buttress is *Central Scoop*, a 350-ft. Grade III climbed by Mr. and Mrs. I. S. Clough, also in March 1969.

BIBLIOGRAPHY

Climbers' Guide to Glencoe and Ardgour, Volume 1 (Buchaille Etive Mòr) and Volume 2 (Glencoe, Beinn Trilleachan and Garbh Bheinn). L. S. Lovat. (S.M.C. 1959 and 1965.)

Scottish Mountaineering Club Journal, Nos. 151 to 161.

Mountaineering in Scotland, W. H. Murray. (Dent. 1947.)

Undiscovered Scotland, W. H. Murray. (Dent. 1951.)

A Progress in Mountaineering, J. H. B. Bell. (Oliver and Boyd. 1950.)

Always a Little Further, Alastair Borthwick. (John Smith. 1969.)

Mountaineering in Britain, Ronald W. Clark and Edward C. Pyatt. (Phoenix House. 1957.)

Highways and Byways in the West Highlands, Seton Gordon. (Macmillan. 1935.)

Glencoe, John Prebble. (Secker and Warburg. 1966.)

Glencoe and Dalness. Illustrated Guide Book. (The National Trust for Scotland.)

7

Beinn a' Bheithir

(1) *Sgòrr Dhearg (3362 ft.). 2½ miles south of Ballachulish Ferry.
(2) Sgòrr Bhan (3104 ft.). ⅓ mile E.N.E. of (1).
(3) *Sgòrr Dhonuill (3284 ft.). 1 mile W. by S. of (1).
(4) Fraochaidh (2883 ft.). 3½ miles E.S.E. of Duror Station.

The beautiful mountain group of Beinn a' Bheithir – or, as it is pronounced, 'Ben Vair' – is situated on the south side of Loch Leven, near its junction with Loch Linnhe. Its formation is that of a great horseshoe, sweeping round from the outlying nose of Beinn Bhan above West Laroch village to the shoulder of Creag Ghorm, which drops steeply to the loch-side one mile west of Ballachulish Ferry.

In recent years the one hindrance to full enjoyment of the group has been the thick screen of woodlands defending the lower slopes. As the trees have grown, so have the tales of difficulties encountered, with ice-axes used as machetes or tempers frayed in serpentine writhings down sunken watercourses to escape the branches. In all fairness, however, it should be added that the forest roads provide a variety of low-level walks – their popularity encouraged by the Forestry Commission – with a Tyrolean atmosphere that is enhanced by occasional fine glimpses of Loch Leven.

One road in particular is worth noting. Half a mile west of the ferry the turn signposted 'Ballachulish Forest' may be taken and in another ½ mile the car left at a garage and road fork. The road thereafter follows right up the west side of Gleann a' Chaolais almost to the forest boundary, then returns down the east side, to contour at 300 ft. round the shoulder of Sgòrr Dhearg and drop back to the main road beside the Episcopal Church. The details are worth bearing in mind if tempers are to be spared, perhaps late in the day.

Probably the most enjoyable expedition on Beinn a' Bheithir is to start at the eastern tip of the horseshoe, climbing from West Laroch –

without any initial afforestation difficulties – the narrow but regular ridge with steep corries on both sides, which leads up to **Sgòrr Bhan** (3104 ft.). Thereafter one can enjoy a delightful high-level walk with some of the most magnificent views in Scotland, from Glencoe, the Mamores and Ben Nevis to Ardgour and Morvern and right down the wide avenue of Loch Linnhe to the Firth of Lorne and beyond.

Farther round, the north-east ridge of Sgòrr Bhan is short and steep, joining the north ridge just mentioned about $\frac{1}{4}$ mile north of the summit. It is of slaty rock, which forms ledges dipping across the ridge from north to south. Near the top the ridge is narrow, with one steep pitch which can be turned by ledges on the south.

If Sgòrr Bhan is being omitted from the round, a particularly enjoyable alternative is to climb **Sgòrr Dhearg** (3362 ft.) by its narrow north ridge. The forest road may be followed westwards from the church for $\frac{1}{2}$ mile, when the intervening screen of conifers becomes sufficiently thin to allow easy access to the moor above. On the descent a helpful aiming-point is the islet at the back of the bay immediately east of North Ballachulish Hotel.

From Sgòrr Dhearg a well-defined ridge drops down W.S.W. to the bealach (2450 ft.), whence, if desired, it is an easy descent into Gleann a' Chaolais past the sharp little horn of Sgòrr a' Chaolais (2700 ft.), so conspicuous in the middle of the horseshoe. To reach the forest road here with least difficulty, follow the burn which drops down the centre of the corrie.

The 800-ft. climb from the bealach to the rocky dome of **Sgòrr Dhonuill** (3284 ft.) is fairly steep but perfectly straightforward. The descent beyond is more gentle and may be continued, bending north and north-east, along the humpy ridge to Creag Ghorm. From here in descent it is advisable to keep westwards towards the old Kentallen Station in order to avoid the worst of the woods.

This arm of the horseshoe may also be used on the ascent if Sgòrr Dhonuill is being approached directly. It is best to follow the forest road right up the glen, then climb due west to the lowest notch on the Creag Ghorm ridge at 2200 ft. – the exit to the plateau straight ahead being considerably steeper. From the notch the ridge rises to just over 2650 ft., then dips again before the final 700 ft. to the summit.

The burn which rises on this plateau ridge $\frac{3}{4}$ mile west of Sgòrr Dhonuill and flows south-west into the River Duror is reported to have a gorge which provides a good rock-scramble. Otherwise there is no record of any rock-climbing on Beinn a' Bheithir.

Fraochaidh (2883 ft.), which lies $2\frac{1}{2}$ miles S.S.W. of Sgòrr Dhonuill, is most easily reached by way of Glen Duror. There is a network of roads in Glenduror Forest and permission to use a car may be sought at the Forestry Commission office near Achindarroch Farm. If obtained, this will allow either an easier approach to the straightforward north-west or north-east ridges of Fraochaidh, or else, if Sgòrr Dhonuill is the objective, uplift through the woods to almost 1000 ft.

Glen Duror may also be pleasantly followed on a 7-mile walk through the hills to Ballachulish, joining the path from Glen Creran above the partially dried reservoir on the Allt Eilidh, or alternatively the choice may be to turn south here to Loch Creran itself.

BIBLIOGRAPHY

Highways and Byways in the West Highlands, Seton Gordon. (Macmillan. 1935.)

8

Glencoe – North side

(1) **Beinn a' Chrulaiste** (2805 ft.). 1½ miles north-west of Kingshouse Hotel.
(2) **Am Bodach** (3085 ft.). 1½ miles north-west of the Meeting of the Three Waters, Glencoe.
(3) ***Meall Dearg** (3118 ft.). ½ mile W.N.W. of (2).
(4) **Stob Coire Lèith** (3080 ft.). ¾ mile W. by N. of (3).
(5) ***Sgòr nam Fiannaidh** (3168 ft.). 1¼ miles north-east of Clachaig Inn.
(6) **Garbh Bheinn** (2835 ft.). 1½ miles south-west of Kinlochleven.

Complementary to the magnificent hills on the south side of Glencoe is the eight-mile barrier to the north, reaching from Beinn a' Chrulaiste in the east to the Pap of Glencoe in the west. Of this by far the most dramatic section is the well-named Aonach Eagach – 'notched ridge' – which, strictly speaking, lies between Am Bodach and Stob Coire Lèith. Seen from the floor of the glen, its jagged saw-edge of towers and pinnacles issues an irresistible invitation; it is in fact the narrowest and one of the most exhilarating ridges on the whole Scottish mainland. The traverse provides a memorable expedition in either direction, although it is made more often from east to west in order to benefit by the higher starting-point (a difference of 400 ft.) and also to enjoy the particularly fine sequence of views out towards the west.

Beinn a' Chrulaiste (2805 ft.) is not an attractive hill in itself although a splendid viewpoint from which to study the intricate lines of buttress and gully on the face of the Buachaille opposite and to look north-eastwards or eastwards to the Blackwater Reservoir and out across the expanse of Rannoch Moor. On Stob Beinn a' Chrulaiste, the lower, western shoulder opposite Lagangarbh Hut, some rock-climbing has been recorded – *The Three Pitches*, 150 ft., very difficult, and *The Strip*, 300 ft., difficult.

Immediately to the west is the Devil's Staircase, the celebrated pass over the hills from Kinlochleven. This was the usual route taken by the drovers and their cattle from Skye and Lochaber, and formed too a part of the old military road between Stirling and Fort William, constructed in 1750–1752. Later, between 1904 and 1909, when the Blackwater Reservoir was being made, there were many among the thousands of navvies who found it a convenient crossing to the hard liquor at Kingshouse. Nowadays it is more familiar as one of the motor-cycle test hills included in the Scottish Six Days Trial.

From Kinlochleven a rough road climbs pleasantly round the wooded mouth of Coire Mhorair to the pipeline penstock at 1000 ft., where a still rougher track, more suggestive of the droving days, branches off and in another $2\frac{1}{4}$ miles of moorland reaches the top of the Staircase (1850 ft.). The descent beyond, at first by a succession of hairpins, then less steeply, eventually runs out through the small wood of conifers at Altnafeadh.

Westwards again from the Staircase the northern ramparts of Glencoe rise gradually for some 3 miles, at first with little hint of the good things in store on the Aonach Eagach itself. The only actual climbing route recorded before Am Bodach is reached is a gully on the south-east face of A'Chailleach.

> *Red Funnel Gully.* 500 ft. Very difficult. (J. G. Parish, T. Graham Brown and R. Fox. August 1950.) Beyond the straight section of road across the summit of the pass, the old road is followed to a bridge and the hillside climbed obliquely for some 500 ft. to the start of the climb. Six moderate pitches are followed by the Red Funnel pitch (90 ft. to belay), where the route ascends slabby rock and heather ledges to the left of a waterfall. An airy traverse right, round a nose, finishes with an awkward pull-up on the far side. Pitch 9 is a deep cave with an easy exit and Pitch 11, the last, a 100-ft. groove. The finish is near a prominent nose of rock well seen on the skyline when looking down Glencoe from Lagangarbh.

Am Bodach (3085 ft.). – The start of the Aonach Eagach proper is reached by a climb at a steep but even gradient from the cottage $\frac{1}{2}$ mile down the glen from the Meeting of the Three Waters.

The traverse of the ridge, which dates from August 1895 (A. R. Wilson, A. W. Russell and A. Fraser), is graded officially as easy, but this unfortunately can be deceptive and the expedition should certainly not be undertaken by any party lacking rock-climbing experience. To a competent party a rope may give useful practice in

85

18. Aonach Eagach.

moving fast together; to those less experienced it is indispensable.

In winter conditions the expedition becomes even more exhilarating and worth-while; also, of course, it becomes a more serious undertaking, often with the need for much step-cutting and occasionally with the hazard of double cornices west of the pinnacles. The most difficult part is usually the descent from Am Bodach.

Under snow especially, the traverse may take considerably longer than expected and more than one party has been overtaken by darkness. The walls, however, are steep and treacherous and almost without exception it is far better to complete the ridge and descend from either end than to succumb to the temptation of chancing any attractive-looking escape route. Especially is this true in winter. The only exception – and it is not recommended – is a wide scree-filled gully which comes down to Achtriochtan immediately to the east of Meall Dearg. There are no pitches, but the scree is the worst kind possible and any enticement it may have is best forgotten.

The most interesting part of the ridge lies between **Meall Dearg** (3118 ft.) and **Stob Coire Lèith** (3080 ft.). Here there are two short pinnacles offering some enjoyable rock-scrambling though avoidable if necessary on the south side. Beyond the Stob it is an easy walk to the fourth and final top, **Sgòr nam Fiannaidh** (3168 ft.). The descent from here, by screes and grass, leads easily though steeply down into the glen, either towards Loch Achtriochtan or farther round towards Clachaig Inn. If the latter line is followed, care should be taken to avoid the deep gash of Clachaig Gully. A further alternative may be to continue for the extra $1\frac{1}{2}$ miles to the excellent viewpoint of Sgòr na Ciche, the Pap of Glencoe (2430 ft.).

Just over 1 mile N.N.E. of Meall Dearg is the outlying **Garbh Bheinn** (2835 ft.), a fine sharp-pointed peak above Loch Leven, conspicuous from both east and west. Apparently it was in its fastnesses that Alan Breck and David Balfour, in R. L. Stevenson's *Kidnapped*, lay hidden after their adventures in Glencoe.

On the Glencoe side of the Aonach Eagach the buttresses are for the most part too vegetatious and rotten to afford any satisfactory rock-climbing. The imposing buttress on Am Bodach, *Chancellor Buttress*, best seen from the road $\frac{3}{4}$ mile west of the Meeting of the Three Waters, is not exceptional in this respect, although providing a 600-ft. difficult route (Morley Wood, A. S. Piggott and J. Wilding. September 1920). Vegetatious, loose and open to variation, the most difficult section is in the middle, while a shattered arête connects the final tower to the summit ridge. In winter the principal difficulty is route-finding at mid-height, after which the crest is regained in two pitches, the second 'about severe'. (W. Skidmore.)

Also on Am Bodach, *Chancellor Gully* affords an excellent severe route of some 1750 ft. (J. F. Hamilton, T. D. MacKinnon, G. S. Roger and C. R. Steven. July 1949.) It is easily distinguishable by the slanting square-cut chimney which hangs above it at mid-height and was first climbed after a very necessary period of drought. The first five pitches are vegetatious in parts and wet, but thereafter the rock becomes clean and sound – notably on the succession of long slab pitches which characterise the middle section.

The first gully left of Chancellor Gully, fading out some 700 ft. above the road, has given a Grade III winter climb with four short ice pitches – *Chance* (G. Anderson and A. J. Trees. February 1969.)

At the other end of the ridge, *Clachaig Gully* is situated directly in front of Clachaig Inn on the south flank of Sgòr nam Fiannaidh, which it splits from top to bottom for 1735 ft. Attracting keen attention since the first exploration in 1894 by Professor Norman Collie's party, it was eventually climbed in May 1938 after three weeks of fine weather (W. H. Murray, A. M. MacAlpine, J. K. W. Dunn and W. G. Marskell). With its 30 pitches, this is one of the finest gully climbs in the country and considerably more exacting than its 'very difficult' grading would suggest. It has a profusion of trees and vegetation on its walls as far as the Great Cave, about 500 ft. up, beyond which the walls become barer and narrower and the climbing harder. Average time for the climb is 3 to 5 hours. In a winter ascent in January 1952 (R. Hope and H. MacInnes) the difficulties of the gully were found to be very severe and the time taken was 5 hours.

BIBLIOGRAPHY

Climbers' Guide to Glencoe and Ardgour, Volume 2. L. S. Lovat. (S.M.C. 1965.)

Mountaineering in Scotland, W. H. Murray. (Dent. 1947.) (Aonach Eagach; Clachaig Gully.)

British Crags and Climbers, Ed. Edward C. Pyatt and Wilfrid Noyce. (Dennis Dobson. 1952.) (Chancellor Gully.)

9

The Mamores

(1) *Mullach nan Coirean (3077 ft.). 5 miles S.S.E. of Fort William.
(2)　Mullach nan Coirean, S.E. top (3004 ft.). ¾ mile south-east of (1).
(3) *Stob Bàn (3274 ft.). 1 mile east of (2).
(4) *Sgùrr a' Mhaim (3601 ft.). 1¼ miles north-east of (3).
(5)　Sgòr an Iubhair (3300 ft.). ¾ mile south of (4).
(6) *Am Bodach (3382 ft.). ¾ mile E.S.E. of (5).
(7) *Stob Coire a' Chairn (3219 ft.). ¾ mile north-east of (6).
(8)　An Garbhanach (3200 ft.). ⅓ mile N.N.E. of (7).
(9) *An Gearanach (3200 ft.). ⅓ mile north of (8).
(10) *Na Gruagaichean (3442 ft.). 2½ miles north-east of Kinlochleven.
(11)　Na Gruagaichean, N.W. top (3404 ft.). ¼ mile north-west of (10).
(12) *Binnein Mòr (3700 ft.). 1 mile N.N.E. of (10).
(13)　Binnein Mòr, S. top (3475 ft.). ½ mile south of (12).
(14) *Binnein Beag (3083 ft.). 1 mile N.N.E. of (12).
(15)　Sgùrr Eilde Beag (3140 ft.). ½ mile south-east of (13).
(16) *Sgùrr Eilde Mòr (3279 ft.). 1 mile north of Loch Eilde Mòr.
(17)　Mam na Gualainn (2603 ft.). 4¼ miles E.N.E. of Ballachulish Ferry.
(18)　Glas Bheinn (2587 ft.). 4¾ miles E.N.E. of Kinlochleven.
(19)　Leum Uilleim (2971 ft.). 2 miles south-west of Corrour Station.

This group of fine mountains lies between Glen Nevis on the north and Loch Leven and Loch Eilde Mòr on the south. The main backbone of the massif runs east and west for some 7 miles, throwing out a series of lesser ridges to the north, the peaks being mostly bold and picturesque and the ridges themselves narrow and well defined.

With the exception of Mullach nan Coirean, which is granite, the Mamores are of mica-schist and quartzite, a hard crystalline rock breaking up into angular fragments that form loose screes on the upper slopes. In distant views the quartzite is often mistaken for snow, as for instance on Sgùrr a' Mhaim and Stob Bàn, where the higher slopes look almost white in certain lights. The name of the latter means, of course, 'white mountain'.

It is a district particularly well suited to ridge-wandering and numerous delightful circuits can be made. For the most part the height keeps above the 2750-ft. contour, dropping in only three places below 2500 ft.: between Stob Bàn and Sgòr an Iubhair (2450 ft.); between Binnein Mòr and Binnean Beag (2450 ft.), and between Sgùrr Eilde Mòr and Sgùrr Eilde Beag (2350 ft.).

The complete traverse of all the tops makes one of the finest hill-walking expeditions in Scotland, while the following formidable marathon, accomplished in June 1964 by the late Philip Tranter, is especially worthy of mention. Leaving Polldubh in Glen Nevis at 3.30 on Saturday afternoon, Tranter and a friend traversed all the Mamores, then descended north from Sgùrr Eilde Mòr, crossed the Allt Coire Rath and climbed Stob Bàn to Stob Choire Claurigh. Four tops farther west, at Stob Coire an Laoigh, Tranter's friend left him to return to Glen Nevis, but Tranter himself continued over the remainder of the Grey Corries, the Aonachs and Càrn Mòr Dearg to the top of Ben Nevis, arriving back at Polldubh on Sunday at 2.45 p.m., having completed a circuit of some 36 miles, with approximately 20,000 ft. of climbing.

The track which skirts the south-western and western flanks of the Mamores was used for centuries by the cattle-drovers on their long, slow treks from Skye and Lochaber to the busy trysts of the South. Stances at Blarmachfoldach and the head of Loch Leven would provide welcome resting-places before the climb over the Devil's Staircase to Altnafeadh. The same route was used for the military road to Fort William. Nowadays, however, the track is little frequented – except by the motor-cycling enthusiasts during the Scottish Six Days Trial – and it is usually by way of Glen Nevis that the western tops of the Mamores are approached.

Up until the turn of the century Kinlochleven was a place of no great consequence. Pennant, passing through on his Highland tour in September 1769, gives it a line or two of commendation: 'Breakfast at the little village of Kinloch-Leven on most excellent minced stag, the only form I thought that animal good in.' Apart from the Devil's Staircase, the only access to it was by a poor road from Fort William or, from Glencoe village, by rough track or boat. Then, between 1904 and 1909, construction of the Blackwater Reservoir took place and the invasion of some thousands of navvies brought a period of the wildest lawlessness. Heavy drinking, brawling and gambling gave 'Aluminiumville' (as it very nearly came to be called) the semblance of some gold-rush town of the Klondike, and it was only when production at the British Aluminium Company's factory fairly got under way in 1908 that the place began to sober down into one of the busiest and hardest-working communities of the Highlands.

On the opposite side of the hills Glen Nevis affords many contrasts, pastoral in its lower stretch, with the sides of the river beautifully wooded, and in no way hinting at the rugged grandeur of the
higher reaches. The glen also has the attraction of offering several
low-level climbing areas, of considerable interest in themselves and
particularly worthy of visits when bad weather puts the high tops out
of condition.

Some amusement may be found in *Achintee Gully* on the side of
Meall an t-Suidhe above Achintee Farm; more probably in the
gullies on the slopes which drop down to the glen above the old grave-
yard from the col between Ben Nevis and Càrn Dearg, S.W. Much the
most interesting of the latter is *Surgeon's Gully*, a very severe climb of
1500 ft. and 21 pitches which, surprisingly, appears to have attracted
very little attention.

Most enjoyable, however, is the excellent low-level climbing to be
had on the Polldubh Crags farther up the glen. Past Achriabhach,
where the road crosses the river at the Lower Falls of Glen
Nevis, one is confronted by these crags near the foot of the
steep slope opposite. They have a frontage of nearly ½ mile and,
facing south, receive what sunshine there is. They are easily accessible from the road and provide some 50 routes of up to 500 ft.
in length, varying in standard from moderate to very severe,
and fully deserving the popularity which has now crowded upon
them.

The Crags originally attracted attention in 1945, the first of the
popular routes being pioneered the following year, and by 1947 the
area had become 'the summer evening rendezvous of the entire
Lochaber mountaineering brotherhood'. Some years later Polldubh
became a favourite training ground for the R.A.F. Mountain Rescue
teams and soon many fine routes of high standard had been worked
out. The severities of the earliest half-dozen climbs were downgraded
as new discoveries were made, such as the two quite short but impressive 'very severes' on Styx Buttress in 1958, *Damnation* and *Dooms-
day*. Then, in the late spring of 1959, more than two dozen new routes
were added, including the longest on the Crags, *Crag Yough Groove*
(500 ft. very severe) by I. S. Clough and T. Sullivan (through leads.)
Now combinations of routes have been found to afford as much as
1000 ft. of climbing of continuously high standard, while with a little
imagination linked routes of less exacting grades can also be worked

out. (For full details see S.M.C. *Climbers' Guide to Ben Nevis*, 1969.)

Beyond Polldubh the road climbs gradually on the right bank of the river to 450 ft. at the car turning-place, 7 miles from Fort William. Above this point is the famous Nevis gorge, about 1 mile in length. Shut in by the south-eastern flanks of Ben Nevis on the one hand and by the complex ramparts of Sgùrr a' Mhaim on the other, the gorge has been justly described as Himalayan rather than Alpine and is altogether unique in Britain. High above the river, this part of the path – described by one writer as 'the most thrilling mile in Scotland' – cuts impressively through to the upper reaches of the glen, at first narrowly enclosed near Steall, site of the J.M.C.S. hut, then widening into open, desolate moorland.

Beyond the gorge and opposite the hut rise the slopes of Meall Cumhann. Some crags on this face – easily reached from the path – offer several routes including two 'very difficults', *Galax* and *Toadal*.

The River Nevis itself, about 14 miles long, rises on the eastern slopes of Binnein Mòr, while beyond the remarkably narrow watershed the Amhainn Rath leads down in another 5 miles to the head of Loch Treig. The walk through to Corrour Station – 22 miles from Fort William – is a particularly fine cross-country expedition, although one that is best tackled in dry conditions. The friendliness of warm sunshine and far views can be almost unbelievably different from the hostility of wind and rain to be met with sometimes on the open moor, with every burn foaming white in spate. The section from Steall to Luibeilt, trackless in places, is apt to be heavy going, although the final 4 miles are easier, with a good if muddy track from Creaguaineach Lodge to the station.

Mullach nan Coirean (3077 ft.) – Situated at the western end, this is the flattest and probably the least interesting of the Mamores. The summit plateau is very extensive and the south-east top (3004 ft.), denoted by a small contour, is difficult to locate in mist. The main top is more definite and the north and north-east ridges are useful guides to it. The latter makes a good approach-route with fine views to Stob Bàn and Sgùrr a' Mhaim, both of which may be included in an enjoyable round from Polldubh. Unfortunately the lower slopes are made difficult by afforestation, and above the forestry roads it is best to follow the line of one of the burns where the trees fall back and allow sufficient room for movement.

Stob Bàn (3274 ft.), one of the features of the view up Glen Nevis, is a beautiful cone-shaped mountain with a distinctive quartzite top. The usual line of ascent is from Polldubh up the north ridge, on which is a very prominent top (2950 ft.) about ⅓ mile short of the summit and apt, in bad weather, to be mistaken for the highest point. Another route is up the south-west ridge from Tigh-na-sleubhaich, on the watershed (1100 ft.) of the old Kinlochleven-Fort William road, but high up the quartzite screes are particularly tiresome. As a further alternative there is a path from Glen Nevis up the Allt Coire a' Mhusgain, under the south ridge of Sgùrr a' Mhaim, to the Stòb Bàn-Sgòr an Iubhair bealach.

The north-east face of Stob Bàn is precipitous and there is some climbing to be had on the main buttresses.

In April 1895 the north buttress gave Tough, Brown, Douglas and Hinxman a good climb, finishing on the 2950-ft. top, while in 1969 J. Grieve and C. MacNaughton made a Grade IV winter route of 1000 ft. on the north-east buttress, starting on its left in the left-hand of two steep chimneys.

The central buttress has a steep triangular lower face. The slanting ridge to the left of this, between two gullies, was climbed by J. Maclay and Parr in January 1904. The rocks were slabby and outward-sloping, 1½ hours being taken for the 200 ft. to the top of the lower buttress. From there to the summit ridge was easy.

The south buttress, directly under the summit, is split by a very obvious gully just to the south of the highest point and is separated from the central buttress by another conspicuous gully. This summit buttress was explored in April 1948 by J. C. Henderson, D. Scott and R. Anderson and also by G. Allison and J. G. Black. The obvious gully proved to be quite easy, but a good route was worked out starting at the foot of the buttress and going up 150 ft. of steep and difficult rock and finishing a few yards from the summit cairn. Allison and Black did a more difficult variation to the left on the lower steep rocks. The gully between the summit buttress and the central buttress was glissaded.

Sgùrr a' Mhaim (3601 ft.) – This is the second highest top in the Mamores. Its huge mass fills up the head of Glen Nevis and its beautiful little cup-shaped north corrie is a conspicuous feature in the view south from Ben Nevis. The usual line of ascent is from Polldubh up the north-west ridge.

From Steall, the north-east ridge may be climbed without difficulty, or else, more interestingly, one can cut south across the little north-east corrie to the east ridge. This gives a good scramble of 800 ft. up to a rocky pinnacle near the main north-east ridge beyond which the finish is narrow.

The spur which drops north-westwards from the north-east ridge of Sgùrr a' Mhaim – Creag Uaimh Shomhairle – has recently been found to offer some good climbing. Seen from the turning-place at the end of the Glen Nevis road, it may be reached in about 15 minutes by crossing the river and climbing steeply to the foot of the spur. The crag, which has several further possibilities of high-standard new routes, is steep and overhanging in places, and is some 300 ft. high and 150 yards long. Unfortunately, it faces north-west and so only receives sunshine in the evening; it tends to be greasy in wet weather and does not dry out quickly.

Sunset Boulevard. 300 ft. Severe. (I. Clough, Miss J. Davis, J. Gargett, R. Matthews and D. Ducker. March 1960.) Start near centre of crag at a quartz blaze, right of an overhang and left of a tall light-coloured wall. (1) 60 ft. Climb steeply up wall for 15 ft. on good holds to ledge; traverse left, climb a scoop and move left again to holly tree; chockstone belay. (2) 70 ft. Up by crack and wall, past next tree to a groove; climb this to tree belays. (3) 70 ft. Up chimney in corner above; traverse almost horizontally left to grass and trees in overhung bay. (4) 100 ft. Up right to corner; piton runner used. Step delicately round on to nose of rib on right, and more delicately into vegetatious chimney; up this to belay. Scrambling remains.

Sundowner. 220 ft. Severe. (I. Clough, Miss J. Davis, J. Gargett, R. Matthews and D. Ducker. March 1960.) Start on right of crag, at a tree and an arrow. (1) 30 ft. Up, trending left, to small stance and belay above overhang. (2) 60 ft. To birch tree terrace; delicate last moves. (3) 80 ft. Diagonally right, up to steep wall; climb this direct or by a turning movement on right. Either way arrive at sapling. Thence traverse left along ledge and climb groove to flake belay. (4) 50 ft. Up slab on right, then straight up wall above; flake belay on left.

The south ridge of Sgùrr a' Mhaim is sometimes called the Devil's Ridge. Under deep snow and heavily corniced it has a formidable appearance, and although no more than an exhilarating walk it should be treated with respect. About ½ mile along the ridge there is a small shapely peak marked by the 3250-ft. contour and known as Stob Coire a' Mhail.

Sgòr an Iubhair (3300 ft.). This top stands at the junction of the Sgùrr a' Mhaim south ridge and the main ridge. It is not named on the one-inch O.S. map, but is denoted by a small 3250-ft. contour.

Three Fingers. 100 ft. Very difficult. On the best-looking piece of slab below and slightly to the right of the top, well seen from Am Bodach. Start at the left end of the slab and follow the line of least resistance to the top.

Am Bodach (3382 ft.). This peak is well seen from Loch Leven, although the finest view of it is from Sgùrr a' Mhaim. From the saddle to the west (2800 ft.) a path runs down into Coire na h-Eirghe, crossing to the right bank of the burn at about 2400 ft. and continuing down to the old road 2 miles from Kinlochleven.

Kinlochleven is the best centre for all the Mamore peaks from Am Bodach eastwards. A private road leaves the main A82 half a mile west of the village and climbs past Mamore Lodge (650 ft.) to Lochs Eilde Mòr and Beag and thence to Luibeilt. This road is suitable for ordinary cars as far as the cottage just above the Lodge, but beyond that for Land-Rovers only. Permission to use it is, however, necessary from the tenant at the Lodge.

Also most useful is the good footpath which follows a more direct line upwards from Kinlochleven to join the Loch Eilde Mòr road ½ mile west of the loch itself. The path then contours round Sgùrr Eilde Beag to reach and cross the bealach with the lochans immediately west of Sgùrr Eilde Mòr (the best route, referred to below, from Kinlochleven to Binnein Beag). A branch of this path leads also to the ridge between the south top of Binnein Mòr and Sgùrr Eilde Beag.

The old track to Fort William starts just west of the village and runs north-west, crossing the lower part of the road to the Lodge.

Stob Coire a' Chairn (3219 ft.). This peak, unnamed on the one-inch map, stands on the main ridge at its junction with the subsidiary ridge to An Garbhanach and An Gearanach. The col to the south-west is about 2800 ft. and that to the south-east 2555 ft., both saddles being crossed by paths coming up from the Allt Coire na Bà.

An Gearanach (3200 ft). This is the end of a well-defined wall-like ridge which runs northwards for about 600 yards from **An Garbhanach** (3200 ft.). It would appear that the northerly summit is the higher of the two. The connecting ridge is exceptionally narrow and grassy apart from its southern end, which is rocky. Between these outliers and the main ridge the saddle is 2800 ft. and from it An Garbhanach presents a fine, bold appearance, although the rocks are too broken up and indefinite to provide any real climbing. From An Gearanach a descent may be made to Steall by the north-west ridge.

Na Gruagaichean (3442 ft.) is rather a featureless mountain with two tops ¼ mile apart and separated by a dip of 200 ft. If it is being climbed on its own, perhaps the best route is to take the path up Coire na Bà to the 2555-ft. bealach north-west of the lower top and from there follow the ridge over both tops and descend by the south ridge.

Binnein Mòr (3700 ft.). This is the highest mountain in the Mamore forest and also the most outstanding. From the north and from the south it appears as a graceful sharp-pointed peak; from the east and from the west it rises up as a great clean-cut wedge. Steep slopes of quartzite screes run down on all sides. The summit ridge runs north and south for ½ mile, with the highest point at one end and the south top (3475 ft.) at the other, lying on the main ridge itself.

The best route of ascent is probably over Na Gruagaichean, the intervening bealach being 3100 ft., although the path to the dip in the ridge south-east of the south top is a good alternative. From Steall, after being rather shut in to begin with, the route up the N.N.W. ridge is very enjoyable, with the views of the Grey Corries, the Aonachs and Ben Nevis widening to a fine panorama at the summit.

Binnein Beag (3083 ft.). A symmetrical, cone-shaped little hill with steep quartzite screes on all sides. If it is being climbed along with Binnein Mòr, the latter's N.N.W. ridge may be found to be a preferable link to the steep N.N.E. ridge, which is broken and loose and, in places, slabby and mossy. From Kinlochleven the excellent path over the Sgùrr Eilde Mòr bealach will be found a pleasant approach-route.

Sgùrr Eilde Beag (3140 ft.) – A doubtful top, as the drop between it and Binnein Mòr's south summit is almost imperceptible. The path which runs up to this dip from the south is a convenient way of approach; the eastern slopes drop steeply for some 750 ft. to the broad saddle with the lochans.

Sgùrr Eilde Mòr (3279 ft.) – This is a broad flat-topped mountain, like Mullach nan Coirean at the other end of the range. It can be climbed easily from the road at Loch Eilde Mòr (1122 ft.), or by way of the path to the lochans. The northern ridge is broad and slopes gently down towards the watershed between the Nevis and the Amhainn Rath. It ends in a conspicuous top, Meall Doire na h-Achlais (2150 ft.).

Two miles south-east of Sgùrr Eilde Mòr on the opposite side of the lochs, **Glas Bheinn** (2587 ft.) is the highest point of a ridge running south-west to north-east. Still farther east the bulkier massif culminating in **Leum Uilleim** (2971 ft.) is more easily accessible from Corrour. A path from the station crosses the moor to the far side of the Allt Coir' a' Bhric Beag at about 1600 ft. Thereafter a number of cairns complicate an otherwise simple ascent of the north-east ridge of Beinn a' Bhric (2863 ft.); thence to Leum Uilleim and a pleasant descent by the pronounced nose, Sròn an Lagain Ghairbh. Views of the Blackwater Reservoir, Loch Laidon, Loch Ossian, and Loch Treig in their setting of hill and moor are especially fine.

Reverting to the western end of the group, **Mam na Gualainn** (2603 ft.) is the summit of the ridge flanking the old Fort William road on the south. A fine view-point, it may be climbed steeply from the road along Loch Leven-side or, more gradually, by its north-east ridge from Tigh-na-sleubhaich.

Still farther west the Dubh-Lag crag near Onich (G.R. NN 025620) deserves mention as a recently discovered practice-ground. It is a ¾-mile long slabby wall of quartzite, reaching a height of 300 ft. at points, and is situated almost at sea-level about 100 yards from the

D

main road. Most of the existing routes are around severe standard and average 150 ft. in length.

BIBLIOGRAPHY

Climbers' Guide to Ben Nevis, J. R. Marshall. (S.M.C. 1969.)

10

Ben Nevis

(1) *Ben Nevis (4406 ft.). Lochaber.
(2) Càrn Dearg (S.W.) (3348 ft.). 1 mile south-west of (1).
(3) Càrn Dearg (N.W.) (3961 ft.). ¾ mile north-west of (1).

It is fitting, perhaps, that Ben Nevis, as well as being the highest mountain in Britain, should also be able to lay fair claim to being the most deceptive. To those who know it only from the colour calendars and the postcards, even to a great many of those whose experience of it goes no further than the long zigzags of the pony-track, it is nothing more than a bulky, round-shouldered mass, more often than not wet and misty and unfriendly; it is only to those who care to discover something of its uniqueness of character as snow mountain and rock peak, who acquaint themselves with the two miles of ridge and buttress and gully, the most formidable rock-face in Britain, that it reveals its true stature.

In Blaeu's Great Atlas of 1654, Gordon of Straloch's map of Braid-Allaban, Athol, Brae of Mar, Badenoch, Strath-spey and Lochabyr shows 'Bin Novesh' and 'Glen Nevish' – unfortunately not spelling variants that are in any way helpful as clues to the meaning of the name. This appears to be 'venomous' or 'malicious', an interpretation that is sometimes not unduly difficult to accept.

A good deal of mist also obscures the details of most of the earliest ascents. The following particulars have been taken mainly from Professor D. B. Horn's interesting article 'The Origins of Mountaineering in Scotland' (S.M.C.J. XXVIII, pp. 157–173).

The first recorded ascent seems to have been made in the summer of 1771 by a certain James Robertson, financed by the Commissioners on the Forfeited Estates to bring back botanical specimens from the Highland hills for the Edinburgh University Museum. Three years later another professional – this time a Welshman named John Williams, but again working for the Commissioners – was prospecting on the summit for possible mineral wealth. At about that time the climb must have been beginning to gain in popularity, for when the first recorded tourist ascent occurred in 1787, more than 30 small cairns erected by previous visitors were seen on the summit. This 13-hour expedition is of special interest as it involved the use not only of a rope but also of a mechanical aid in the form of a grappling iron for the rock-climbing encountered *en route*. The party, which had three guides and four soldiers from the Fort William garrison to act as porters, glissaded on their 'haunches' for much of the way down.

One botanist who made an early recorded ascent was James Dickson, his companion being Mungo Park, his brother-in-law and the future explorer of Africa. A tourist visitor in 1800 mentions meeting other parties near the summit, including a Mr. Grant of Glen Urquhart, who 'plied the whiskey bottle with considerable alacrity, but notwithstanding found the descent more perilous and difficult than the ascent', while in 1818, when Keats made his ascent in dense mist, he records that he had been preceded not many years before by 'the fattest woman in all Inverness-shire'. During an ascent between 1836 and 1850 Professor J. D. Forbes made history by cutting the first steps in snow on Ben Nevis.

What may be described as the 'meteorological era' dates from 1877, when the Scottish Meteorological Society considered the possibility of taking daily readings on the summit. In the event this task was undertaken by Mr. Clement Wragge, of Fort William, who made the ascent daily throughout the summer of 1881 and the summer and autumn of 1882. In those days no track existed and the upper part of the climb had to be made over bare scree and rocks – a fact to be borne in mind as one tries to imagine aright something of what was involved in these feats.

Plans were next laid for the building of a summit observatory. A pony-track, costing £800, was made, allowing construction to go ahead, and the observatory was duly opened on October 17, 1883. Built of granite blocks lined with double wooden walls covered with felt, it consisted originally of one apartment 13 ft. square – the living-room and office – with three small bunks, as well as coal cellar etc., opening off it. However, so much trouble was experienced during the first winter, mainly with drifting snow, that the next summer a larger room, two additional bedrooms and a 30-ft. tower were added. Here continuous observations were made, later in co-

19. The pony-track, Ben Nevis.

operation with another observatory at sea-level and periodically half-way up the mountain at a temporary building during certain summer seasons. On October 1, 1904, despite storms of protest in the press, the observatory was closed down.

Many of the records that were collected are extraordinarily interesting, for example the average amount of sunshine which, taken over a year, is only two hours a day. The wettest year was 1898 with a total of 240.12 inches, while the wettest month was December 1900 with 48.34 inches. Only in April, May and June is the monthly rainfall average less than 10 inches. In the worst gales of winter some of the gusts were estimated to exceed 150 m.p.h. Snowfall in the days of the observatory seems to have been much heavier than in recent years, such as 1935, for example, when a visit was paid to all the places on Ben Nevis where snow is known to lie and not a trace could be found. This would have considerably troubled one owner of the past who traditionally held the land so long as snow remained on the mountain. All was well until a winter of little snow was followed by a particularly hot summer and the only way then to save the land was by erecting a tent over an all-important snow-wreath to keep it from melting.

The observatory was later brought into use again as part of the hotel that was opened at the summit, this venture lasting until the end of the First World War, when the buildings were finally allowed to fall into ruin. 'Upon the summit,' states an old guide book of just over 50 years ago, 'are a Temperance Hotel and a building formerly used as an observatory. The charge for luncheon is 3s. and for tea, bed and breakfast 10s. Many persons ascend the Ben in the evening to see the sun rise over the North Sea and light up the vast amphi-theatre of grand mountain tops visible from the summit.' It is interesting to note that at that time permits were being issued for the use of the path: 1s. for each pedestrian and 3s. for each person on horseback, while the charge for a pony and guide was 21s.

During the observatory years Ben Nevis must have been a busy mountain indeed. There was a constant stream of tourist visitors, especially after the opening of the West Highland railway in 1894; there was the regular traffic of the supply-ponies up and down the path; the beginnings of serious climbing may be said to date from 1892, while the well-known Ben Nevis race was started in 1895 – an event which still takes place annually on the first Saturday in September from the King George V Park in Fort William to the summit and back, a distance of approximately 10 miles and with the present almost incredible record, set up in 1964 by Peter Hall of Barrow, standing at 1 hour 38 minutes 50 seconds.

A particularly important event in the history of Ben Nevis was the opening on April 1, 1929 of the Scottish Mountaineering Club hut, presented by Dr. and Mrs. W. Inglis Clark in memory of their son Captain Charles Inglis Clark, who had died in 1918. Situated at about 2200 ft. close to the Allt a' Mhuilinn, just above its junction with the burn from the Lochan na Ciste, the hut has been found by

20. The C.I.C. Hut, Ben Nevis.

countless mountaineers to be an ideal base; indeed it is difficult nowadays to think of climbing – or rescue work – on the cliffs of Ben Nevis without it.

Ben Nevis itself is isolated on all sides except where the long narrow eastern arête, which does not fall below 3475 ft., joins it to Càrn Mòr Dearg. Round rarely visited Coire Eoghainn, bounding the plateau on the south in a long curve to Càrn Dearg, S.W., the walls fall away with continuous steepness; the slope from just below the gorge in Glen Nevis to the summit must be the longest and steepest in the country – 4000 ft. at an average angle of over 35 degrees. To the north-west the outlying top of Meall an t-Suidhe (pronounced approximately 'Melantee') (2322 ft.) forms a broad shoulder beyond the bleak, boggy saddle holding Lochan Meall an t-Suidhe.

The ascent of Ben Nevis by the ordinary route, though tiring, is perfectly simple under the usual summer conditions. Leaving Fort William by the north road, one crosses Nevis Bridge and takes the road on the right to reach Achintee Farm where the pony-track starts. This track climbs across the steep flank of Meall an t-Suidhe to reach the saddle between that top and Càrn Dearg, N.W. Above the lochan, at nearly 2000 ft., it turns back and, after crossing the Red Burn, zigzags up the scree-covered slopes to the summit plateau. Here the path is near the precipices, and, as some of the gullies extend far into the plateau, it is necessary to keep a good look-out in misty weather; in winter and spring, when large cornices may project many feet over the edge, special care should be taken.

From the Youth Hostel in Glen Nevis one crosses the River Nevis and goes straight up the slope of Meall an t-Suidhe to join the pony-track near the first zigzag. The normal tourist time from Achintee to the summit in summer is at least 3 hours, with about 2 hours for the descent.

As is to be expected, the views from the summit of Ben Nevis under favourable conditions are very extensive. Ben Wyvis, over 60 miles to the N.N.E., and the Cairngorms, almost as far to the east, lead round to nearer, more easily identified peaks such as Schichallion, Ben More and Stobinian, Buachaille Etive Mòr, Beinn Laoigh, and the Arrochar hills. Southwards and westwards the islands come into their own – Arran and Jura, Colonsay, Lismore and Mull, Coll, with Tiree behind it, Barra and South Uist, 93 miles distant beyond the Small Isles, the Cuillin behind the Streaps. North-westwards are still more well-known mainland peaks and groups:

Ben Sgriol, the Kintail hills, a glimpse of Torridon, Mam Sodhail and Càrn Eige. Farthest of all in the whole panorama, to the left of Jura the sea is visible and in absolutely clear weather a low line of land may be seen – the coast of Ireland 120 miles away.

To reach the C.I.C. Hut from Achintee, instead of turning back to the right above Lochan Meall an t-Suidhe, one continues north-wards across a stretch of boggy ground, keeping almost level until one reaches an old deer fence. Here a path may be found which descends perhaps 100 ft. and, bearing in a north-easterly direction, contours the steep northerly slopes of Càrn Dearg, N.W. A large boulder, the Lunching Stone, may be observed on the left of the path. Time required from Achintee to the Hut about 2½ hours.

More usually the Hut is reached from the distillery near Lochy Bridge. The main railway line here is crossed and the hillside climbed to the light railway track, which is followed leftwards for a few hundred yards to a small bridge. Turn diagonally up the slope beyond the latter to reach the Allt a' Mhuilinn where it is dammed. Cross here and follow a path on the north-east bank of the burn. Time required about 2 hours.

From Steall, one can follow the Allt Coire Giùbhsachan for a mile or more, then bear north-west to cross the Càrn Mòr Dearg arête and descend into Coire Leis to reach the C.I.C. Hut or the foot of the cliffs, or bear more westwards to reach the summit of Ben Nevis.

The approach to Ben Nevis by way of the Càrn Mòr Dearg arête – and more particularly the descent in the reverse direction from the summit to the arête – is given full attention in Chapter 11. As is stressed there, this route under certain conditions is very subtly dangerous and should be treated with the greatest respect. Also mentioned in Chapter 11 are the six abseil posts available for a rapid descent into Coire Leis and the survival shelter, 400 yards from their foot, for use in emergency.

In addition to the Coire Leis shelter – and like it the respon-sibility of the Lochaber Mountaineering Club – there are two survival shelters on the actual plateau of Ben Nevis. One is located at the summit. The other is on Càrn Dearg, N.W., 250 yards from the summit of the latter on a bearing of 200° (G.R. NN 158719). This is 200 yards north of the top of No. 4 Gully and also on a line of small cairns leading down from the top of the Trident Buttress area to the Red Burn.

These shelters – not unlike miniature Nissen huts – are of metal construction and painted orange to make identification easier both from the ground and from the air. Measuring approximately 6 ft. by 8 ft. and 4 ft. high, they will either sleep three comfortably or shelter eight to ten adults with a squeeze. In emergency the wooden benches which they contain could be lashed together to form a sledge or stretcher.

Summer and winter for more than three-quarters of a century, the north-east face of Ben Nevis has provided some of the finest mountaineering in Britain. The classic rock-routes, for the most part of great length, are always worth repeating; under snow and ice they can become exacting enough to satisfy the most fastidious. Recently, some of the particularly outstanding achievements can only be measured fairly against the north-wall severities of the Alps.

Not surprisingly – apart from the easiest gullies – the great ridges were the first to receive the attention of the pioneers. September 1892 was a month of triumph: on the 3rd J. Hopkinson, E. Hopkinson and B. Hopkinson ascended Tower Ridge to the foot of the Great Tower; on the 4th, accompanied by C. Hopkinson, they descended the whole 1900 ft. of the ridge and the Douglas Boulder; then, on the 6th, they made the first ascent of the North-East Buttress. Tower Ridge was first climbed completely in March 1894 by Professor J. Norman Collie, G. A. Solly and J. Collier; in April 1895 Castle Ridge fell to Collie, W. W. Naismith, G. Thomson and M. W. Travers.

These ridges are the most important landmarks of the whole face. *Castle Ridge* is the first to be reached as one walks up the Allt a' Mhuilinn glen – something of an impostor, as it has a formidable appearance yet offers, in summer, not much more than scrambling. Fully a mile away, as if the farther boundary wall, the *North-East Buttress* rises from the floor of the glen in an imposing rock-curtain. Rated as difficult, it has several awkward sections including the celebrated 'Man-trap', which bars the way high up with a nose of rock about 10 ft. high. In winter this pitch is often found to be the crux of a very long climb and can pose an awkward choice between retreating or forcing a way to easier ground above. If there is good snow-ice on the Orion (north-west) face, the nose can often be turned by traversing the Orion face for 20 ft., ascending a scoop and then traversing back at the level of the top of the nose. Probably the best known and most popular route on the mountain, *Tower Ridge* rises to the east of Coire na Ciste at a level of 2300 ft., only a short distance above the C.I.C. Hut. With or without the introductory

21. North-East Buttress, Ben Nevis. To its right, Zero Gully, Observatory Ridge and Point five Gully.

700 ft. of the *Douglas Boulder*, it is a splendid climb – straightforward in summer; under winter conditions an expedition to exhilarate, tax – and even on occasion defeat – strong parties. Like the North-East Buttress, it has its problems, notably the Great Tower at over 4000 ft. and the Tower Gap beyond.

Two gullies which were probably climbed a number of years earlier than the three great ridges are *No. 3 Gully* and *No. 4 Gully*.

22. Ben Nevis: The Eastern Traverse, Tower Ridge.

In summer both consist of screes; in winter they are usually heavily corniced but provide useful routes of descent from the summit plateau. No. 3 can be identified from above in misty weather by a conspicuous rock pinnacle near its exit. No. 4 forms the lowest col between Ben Nevis and Càrn Dearg, N.W. and as the easiest and safest gully descent, summer or winter, has now been marked by a cairn surmounted by a post bearing a metal plate drilled 'No. 4'.

In the three years 1896, 1897, and 1898, a whole crop of interesting gullies fell as winter climbs to the experts of the day: *No. 2 Gully*, *North* and *South Castle Gullies*, *Tower* and *Gardyloo Gullies* – the last with its snow-tunnel and icefall now a favourite classic – and finally *Moonlight Gully*, which on its first ascent in 1898 needed 9 hours of step-cutting.

In the early years of this century the climbing was dominated by Harold Raeburn, who led no less than 13 first ascents and seconded on a 14th. These included *The Castle* and *Raeburn's Buttress* on Càrn Dearg and three of the *Trident Buttress* routes. Still more important, however, were his ascents of *Observatory Buttress* and, both summer and winter, of *Observatory Ridge*. The latter, a 'difficult' of 900 ft., is now one of the most popular climbs on Ben Nevis, the ordinary, original route starting at the lowest point of the rocks and continuing up the crest of the ridge, bounded on the left by Zero Gully and on the right by Point Five Gully.

Between 1910 and 1930 there was an extraordinary lull during which less than a dozen fresh discoveries were made. Then, in the thirties, a new vigour was born. Dr. G. Graham Macphee, in the course of editing the S.M.C. Climbers' Guide to Ben Nevis from his home base in Liverpool over 300 miles distant, pioneered a score of routes and variations, later, incidentally, while president of the Club, making his hundredth ascent of the mountain. Others were busy too, discovering notably the three delicate ledge and slab severes on *Rubicon Wall* and the 550-ft. *Slav Route*, also severe, on the opposite flank of Zero Gully from Observatory Ridge. Emphasis was now shifting to the formidable north-west wall of the North-East Buttress, a high-level area which Dr. J. H. B. Bell made his own particular preserve, working out, with various partners, his fascinating pattern of *Orion Routes*. During the war the all-too-short career of B. P. Kellett underlined these pointers to the future with some brilliant achievements on rock, notably *Gardyloo Buttress* and *Minus Two Buttress*.

Standards in the quarter-century since the Second World War have reached greater levels still. Curiously, much of the attention in summer has tended to swing to the fierce problems of Càrn Dearg, while the most important winter assaults have been directed to the face and bounding recesses of the North-East Buttress.

Among the former there has been a progression of masterpieces: *Sassenach* in 1954 (J. Brown and D. D. Whillans); *Centurion* and *The Shield* in 1956 (both D. D. Whillans and R. O. Downes); *The*

23. Ben Nevis: The Bullroar, Càrn Dearg.

Bat in 1959 (D. Haston and R. Smith); *The Bullroar* (J. R. Marshall and J. Stenhouse) and *The Orgy* (I. S. Clough and K. Sutcliffe) in 1961; *King Kong* in 1964 (B. W. Robertson, F. Harper and J. Graham), to mention only a selection, yet all very severe and with an average length of some 950 feet.

In winter, the ascent of *Zero Gully* – notable for the excessive steepness and difficulty of the first 400 ft. and reconnoitred many times previously – has been described as 'a big break-through in Nevis climbing . . . a truly great achievement in the history of ice-climbing'. Yet H. MacInnes, A. G. Nicol and T. W. Patey took the remarkably short time of 5 hours on the whole climb in February 1957. Two years later, in January 1959, five days – occupying in all 29 hours of climbing – went to the unique *tour de force* of the first ascent of *Point Five Gully* by J. M. Alexander I. S. Clough, D. Pipes and R. Shaw (alternate leads, alternate days) – a climb which for years had been firing many ambitious plans.

Almost immediately after the pioneering of the latter, a burst of equally inspired activity produced *Minus Two Gully* (J. R. Marshall, J. Stenhouse and D. Haston) and a year later, in February 1960, half a dozen outstanding achievements – all Grade IV or V – by J. R. Marshall and R. Smith and including the fine Orion Face *Direct Route*.

Finally mention may be made of *Route Major*, a 1400-ft. Grade III climb done in February 1969 by I. S. Clough and H. MacInnes on the East Face of the North-East Buttress. The sustained climbing and complicated route-finding, it is claimed, make this one of the most enjoyable routes on the mountain.

BIBLIOGRAPHY

Climbers' Guide to Ben Nevis, J. R. Marshall. (S.M.C. 1969)
Twenty Years on Ben Nevis, W. T. Kilgour. (Gardner. 1905.)
Mountaineering in Scotland, W. H. Murray. (Dent. 1947.)
Undiscovered Scotland, W. H. Murray. (Dent. 1951.)
Mountaineering in Britain, Ronald W. Clark and Edward C. Pyatt. (Phoenix House. 1957.)
A Progress in Mountaineering, J. H. B. Bell. (Oliver and Boyd. 1950.)
Highways and Byways in the West Highlands, Seton Gordon. (Macmillan. 1948.)

24. Mamore Ridges. Sgòr an Iubhair from the Devil's Ridge, Sgùrr a' Mhaim.

11

Càrn Mòr Dearg

(1) *Càrn Mòr Dearg (4012 ft.). $\frac{3}{4}$ mile north-east of Ben Nevis.
(2) Càrn Dearg Meadhonach (3873 ft.). $\frac{1}{2}$ mile N.N.W. of (1).
(3) Càrn Beag Dearg (3264 ft.). 1 mile N.N.W. of (1).

The ridge of Càrn Mòr Dearg lies immediately north-east of Ben Nevis, linking up with the latter in a swing southwards and westwards round the head of Coire Leis. Seen from the Fort William–Spean Bridge road, its broad grassy shoulder and the pink screes which drop from its crest to the Allt a' Mhuilinn glen seem tame and gentle compared with the towering grey rock-face opposite.

Inevitably Càrn Mòr Dearg shares in most of the hostile weather which invades the high plateau of Ben Nevis. On days of driving sleet or level hail, when mist blots out the whole trough of the Allt a' Mhuilinn, its ridge can seem almost as inhospitable as the neighbouring cliffs themselves. On the other hand, when the sun does take command, there is more than generous compensation. Then, probably with wall and buttress thick-plastered with snow, the views from its tops make one of the most striking panoramas to be seen in this country.

The usual route of ascent is from the Allt a' Mhuilinn path to the Charles Inglis Clark Hut, slanting easily from the glen up the north-west slopes to the first top, Càrn Beag Dearg. The latter is really only a shoulder and thereafter a delightful walk of a mile takes one over Càrn Dearg Meadhonach to the cairn of Càrn Mòr Dearg. The summit may also be reached directly from the Hut up some 1800 ft., largely steep scree, or else from Steall, in Glen Nevis, up the Allt Coire Giùbhsachan to the saddle leading to the Aonachs – marked as 2915 ft. on the one-inch O.S. map, although shown by the contour lines to be lower than 2750 ft. – then a further 1300 ft. up a well-defined grassy ridge. The slopes on the eastern side of the mountain fall steeply to the glen of the Allt Daimh.

25. Ben Nevis and the Càrn Mòr Dearg Arête.

The East Buttress of Càrn Dearg Meadhonach consists of a rocky ridge descending to the Allt Daimh from the summit cairn. It is marked by a prominent pinnacle – its top estimated at 3800 ft. – at about two-thirds of its height and a cluster of teeth lower down at about 3700 ft. The teeth and, more particularly, the pinnacle are striking as seen in profile from Càrn Beag Dearg. The pinnacle may be reached from the cairn of Càrn Dearg Meadhonach by descending a steep slope and then broken rocks to a small col, from which an easy scramble of about 20 ft. over very rotten rock leads to its top. The ascent of the whole buttress appears to present no special difficulties other than those occasioned by the looseness of the rock, the section from the teeth to the pinnacle being less formidable than it looks from Càrn Beag Dearg.

The well-known Càrn Mòr Dearg arête, which swings round the head of Coire Leis to Ben Nevis, is a very fine ridge affording some rock-scrambling. The lowest point is 3478 ft., so that the re-ascent to the summit of Ben Nevis is nearly 1000 ft. The walk over the tops of Càrn Mòr Dearg and along the arête, returning over Nevis, is one of the finest high-level expeditions in the country.

In summer the slope leading down from the observatory on Ben Nevis to the arête is broad, easy and safe, although of ankle-breaking scree. Occasionally, however, under certain winter conditions it is subtly deceptive and has been the direct cause of a number of fatal accidents. On either side is a steep declivity: to the north-east the floor of Coire Leis is 1250 ft. below and to the south-west Coire Eoghainn drops for 1500 ft. The slope is in full sun and, by January, after many alternations of freezing and thawing, of snowfall and rainfall and condensation, a tough dark ice may form, in which even the largest boulders are submerged. A smooth, dangerous surface results, too hard to make an impression on, unless with sharp crampons, and deadly in rubber soles.

In descending from the observatory the general direction of the arête is south-east, although at first it is necessary to bear more easterly. If, however, this course is held for too long, even before the edge of the corrie is obvious one may find oneself in difficulties and unable to arrest a slide to Coire Leis; lower down, as the slope eases off, the course is more southerly and here it is necessary to guard against an almost equally subtle slide into Coire Eoghainn.

In order to minimize the risk of accidents, a line of posts and two tripod warning notices marked 'Danger. Keep to the Posts' have been erected. The uppermost notice is 130 yards from the summit cairn on a true bearing of 120° (128° magnetic in 1970), while the posts some 20–30 yards apart, lie on a true bearing of 170° (178° magnetic in 1970).

In the gully which descends into Coire Leis from below the steepest part of the slope six abseil posts at 50-ft. intervals have been provided. There is in addition an orange-painted survival shelter – the responsibility of Lochaber Mountaineering Club – at the foot of the gully (G.R. NN 174713; that is 150 yards above the small lochan marked on the 1-inch O.S. map, or approximately 400 yards north-east from the lowest abseil post). It should be noted, however, that in deep snow the posts may be completely covered over and further – a point which cannot be too forcibly stressed – that this is not an easy escape route in emergency. In the event of difficulty at the summit of Ben Nevis the only safe retreat is by way of the tourist path, at least as far as Lochan Meall an t-Suidhe.

12

The Aonachs

---

(1) *Aonach Mòr (3999 ft.). 2 miles N.E. by N. from Ben Nevis.
(2) Stob an Cul Choire (3580 ft.). ⅔ mile E. by N. of (1).
(3) Stob Coire an Fhir Dhuibh (3250 ft.). 1 mile north-east of (1).
(4) Tom na Sròine (3015 ft.). ½ mile north of (3).
(5) *Aonach Beag (4060 ft.). 2 miles east from Ben Nevis.
(6) Stob Coire Bhealaich (3644 ft.). ½ mile south-east of (5).
(7) Sgùrr a' Bhuic (3165 ft.). 1 mile S.E. by S. of (5).

Like Càrn Mòr Dearg, Aonach Mòr and Aonach Beag pay the penalty of lying too close to Ben Nevis; certainly the attention they receive is less than it would have been otherwise. In addition, they are not easily seen to full advantage, standing well back as they do almost as though anxious to remain austerely aloof.

Yet the two Aonachs are by no means mountains to be ignored. They are the summits of the long ridge which forms the western wall of the immense, lonely cirque of hills draining to the headwaters of the Cour, a fine river which drops in turn to the Spean. This arm which they make is fairly steep on its west side; on the east it is precipitous, falling to corries as deep and remote as any to be found in the Highlands.

Aonach Beag lies about 2 miles directly east of the summit of Ben Nevis, while Aonach Mòr is about 1 mile north of Aonach Beag. The two are connected on the west with Càrn Mòr Dearg by a ridge which starts about midway between them, not clearly marked to begin with but becoming well-defined at its central part.

According to the heights of the two mountains, the names should really have been reversed. Probably it was as the bulkier that Aonach Mòr was given the preference – some compensation for having been surveyed as 3999 ft. and so denied the privilege of joining the select company of 'four thousanders'.

Aonach Mòr (3999 ft.) is seen at its best from Glen Spean –

unforgettably under deep snow, with the sun catching the cornice-line of its plateau against an alpine blue sky. The River Spean, famous for its spectacular, clean-cut gorges – the most notable at Monessie – and its deep black pools where salmon lie, provides the necessary contrast in the foreground.

The actual approach to the mountain is best made from the north, from a point about 2 miles from the west end of the old Fort William–Spean Bridge road. Aiming for the broad north ridge and keeping Sgùrr Finnisg-aig on the left, the old light railway track is crossed at about 600 ft. and another 1500-ft. rise brings the climber into the very shallow corrie with the ridge, Aonach an Nid, on the left. This corrie, facing north, usually carries plenty of snow and holds it well, so that its gentle slopes are admirably suited for ski-ing. Aonach Mòr indeed is a particularly attractive ski-mountain, with the possibility of a continuous descent of more than 3000 ft. at an almost even gradient. Above 3500 ft. the slope becomes a bulky and imposing ridge reminiscent of the Cairngorms, rising almost imperceptibly for $\frac{3}{4}$ mile to the very conspicuous summit cairn.

The three subsidiary tops of Aonach Mòr are all on the long branch ridge running east and north to enclose a deep corrie holding several lochans. To reach, first, **Stob an Cul Choire** (3580 ft.), one goes due east from the Aonach Mòr cairn to the edge of the line of cliffs, then a short distance left to find the way down to the ridge. **Stob an Fhir Dhuibh** (3250 ft.), the second top, lies beyond a short descent and further rise of about 50 ft., while **Tom na Sròine** (3015 ft.) is little more than $\frac{1}{2}$ mile further north. This last name is applied on the map to the termination of the ridge at the 2000-ft. contour, but here is used to refer to the top itself, enclosed in the 3000-ft. contour.

The most prominent buttress in the corrie formed by the south and east ridges of Aonach Mòr – conspicuous when viewed from the Aonach Mòr–Aonach Beag bealach – has provided two roughly parallel climbs. They are easily accessible from the col by moving down leftwards over an area of large scree.

Route 1. 400 ft. Difficult. (J. G. Fraser and K. Anderson. September 1945.) Starting in the centre of the buttress the main difficulties were met early on. Higher, it was occasionally necessary to look deliberately for pitches to prevent the climb degenerating into a steep scramble. A narrow neck, of imposing aspect when seen from below, leads to easier rocks and the summit plateau.

Route 2. 400 ft. Difficult. (V. G. A. Freeman, J. Rutherford and F. Baird. September 1945.) Starting to the right, a pitch of 30 ft. is followed by a short, overhanging face with small holds; this may be avoided by a traverse right to a sloping slab and small grass ledge. Three moderate pitches to a ledge overlooking the gully on the right are followed by a 40-ft. pitch on small but good holds, a crack on the left and a series of faces, broken by ledges.

26. Near the summit of Aonach Beag.

Aonach Beag (4060 ft.) is an imposing-looking mountain, rising with fine sweeping lines from the south to form a great dome, the far side of which is cut away to form a line of cliffs overlooking the headwaters of the Allt a' Chùl Choire. The saddle connecting it with Aonach Mòr is narrow, and the first 100 ft. up to Aonach Beag are steep and rocky, and might give considerable trouble to a party descending under winter conditions in misty weather. The top is flat, with two very small cairns near the edge of the cliffs. The westerly cairn appears to be the actual top.

The best route of approach is from Steall, either up the tributary of the Allt Coire Giùbhsachan and thence directly to the summit, or up the main burn itself to near the saddle leading to Càrn Mòr Dearg; turning east, the Aonach Mòr-Aonach Beag bealach (3600 ft.) is reached, with the north-west ridge thereafter leading steeply then more easily to the summit.

The ridge running south-east from Aonach Beag takes one in ½ mile and with only a small rise to **Stob Coire Bhealaich** (3644 ft.). Another top or buttress, more worthy perhaps of inclusion in Munro's Tables, lies ½ mile farther on, where the ridge turns sharply to the south. This buttress rises steeply for 1100 ft. from the saddle connecting it on the east with Sgùrr Chòinnich Beag and presents an imposing appearance from below. It involves some scrambling and requires care. **Sgùrr a' Bhuic** (3165 ft.) lies about ⅔ mile south of the unnamed buttress, the intervening saddle being about 2960 ft. This is a shapely peak, conspicuous from many points to the east.

North-East Ridge. 1500 ft. Difficult. (J. Maclay, W. W. Naismith and G. Thomson. April 1895). Springing practically from the lip of the upper corrie below the Aonach Mòr–Aonach Beag saddle, the ridge is conspicuous to anyone approaching from the northeast up the long, tortuous valley of the Cour, the Allt Coire an Eòin and the Allt a' Chùl Choire. Its possibilities were noted by Professor Norman Collie before the actual first ascent was made, but for almost fifty years afterwards the ridge was so rarely visited that only two ascents were recorded, in April 1904 and August 1942. Since then, of course, more parties have been to it, but even so its utter remoteness is still one of its chief attractions. In its lower part, the rock is not particularly pleasant for climbing and pitches are avoidable. The middle section, however, is narrower and exposed in places, with several pinnacles, a slab and a 12-ft. overhanging rib providing some good situations. It is possible to walk on to the ridge from the corrie on the east at 3000 ft. and again at 3600 ft., above which it becomes broader and easier. The finish is some 60 yards north-west of the summit.

Three routes on the upper western crags of Aonach Beag have

been recorded and further climbing seems possible there, the rock being hard, brittle schist.

Raw Egg (South-West) Buttress. 550 ft. Difficult. (T. D. Mac-Kinnon, J. A. Brown and B. H. Humble. May 1938.) From the road-end in Glen Nevis the buttress can be seen on the skyline through the gap between Meall Cumhann and the south-eastern slopes of Ben Nevis. It is best approached, however, from Upper Steall by way of the Allt Coire Giùbhsachan. Start by a difficult little chimney to a cave, thereafter zigzagging with a few walking pitches. Finish with a stride across another chimney and steep pull up a vertical crack. There are 11 pitches between 40 and 60 ft., with an escape to the left above the middle section.

Crevassed Rib. 300 ft. Difficult. (Mr and Mrs. G. Scott Johnstone. September 1951.) From Upper Steall a prominent nose is seen on the left upper skyline (Skyline Buttress). About 100 yards beyond this, towards Raw Egg Buttress, is a bay in the cliff with a slabby wall to the south and a chimney to the north. Crevassed Rib, on the south side of the chimney, gives interesting climbing on steep rock with small, incut holds. The formidable upper slab was turned on the inside of the gully.

Northern Buttress. 300 ft. Moderate. (V. Thomas and M. Coventry. September 1951.) On the north side of the chimney. Steep pitches, but not exposed.

BIBLIOGRAPHY

Scottish Mountains on Ski, Malcolm Slesser.
 (West Col, 1970.)

13

The Grey Corries

(1) ***Stob Choire Claurigh** (3858 ft.). $4\frac{1}{2}$ miles south of Roy Bridge.
(2)   **Stob Choire Claurigh, North Top** (3719 ft.). $\frac{1}{3}$ mile north of (1).
(3)   **Stob Coire Gaibhre** (3150 ft.). $1\frac{1}{4}$ miles north of (1).
(4)   **Stob Coire na Ceannain** (3720 ft.). $\frac{1}{3}$ mile north-east of (2).
(5)   **Stob a' Choire Lèith** (3627 ft.). $\frac{1}{3}$ mile W. by S. of (1).
(6) ***Stob Coire an Laoigh** (3659 ft.). $1\frac{1}{4}$ miles south-west of (5).
(7)   **Caisteal** (3609 ft.). $\frac{1}{2}$ mile north-east of (6).
(8)   **Stob Coire Cath na Sine** (3529 ft.). $\frac{1}{2}$ mile E. by N. of (7).
(9)   **Stob Coire an Easain** (3545 ft.). $\frac{1}{4}$ mile north-west of (6).
(10) ***Sgùrr Chòinnich Mòr** (3603 ft.). $\frac{3}{4}$ mile S.S.W. of (9).
(11) **Sgùrr Chòinnich Beag** (3175 ft.). $\frac{1}{2}$ mile south-west of (10).
(12) ***Stob Bàn** (3217 ft.). 1 mile S. by E. of (1).
(13) ***Stob Coire Easain** (3658 ft.). $1\frac{3}{4}$ miles west of Loch Treig.
(14) ***Stob a' Choire Mheadhoin** (3610 ft.). $\frac{2}{3}$ mile north-east of (13).
(15) **Sgùrr Innse** (2600 ft.). $1\frac{1}{2}$ miles north-west of (13).
(16) **Cruach Innse** (2800 ft.). 3 miles S. by E. of Roy Bridge Station.

Under the title of the 'Grey Corries' – an old local name and an apt description on account of their numerous slopes of ash-grey scree – are included the two groups of hills lying between Glen Spean and the headwaters of the Nevis and the Amhainn Rath, and extending eastwards from the Aonachs to Loch Treig. The hills form part of the magnificent panorama so well seen as one drops down to Spean Bridge, driving south past the Commando memorial.

    The groups are separated by the deep trough of the Lairig Leacach, which runs south-eastwards from Spean Bridge to the head of Loch Treig. This pass was sometimes used by the old-time cattle drovers in preference to the more usual road which curved westwards round Ben Nevis from Spean Bridge to the stances at Blarmachfoldach and the head of Loch Leven, then climbed over the Devil's Staircase to Altnafeadh. Today the Lairig Leacach gives the best approach to most of the hills under consideration, either from Spean Bridge or from Corrour. A hill road – negotiable by car from Coire-choille, 2 miles from Spean Bridge on the south side of the river, to the old narrow-gauge railway track – crosses the pass to a bothy 1 mile beyond the watershed (reachable by Land-Rover), where it degenerates into a sheep path for the 3 miles of descent to Creaguaineach.

On the north side of the hills the old Spean Bridge–Fort William road gives an approach to the western summits. The south-west end of the group is best reached from Steall, although from farther to the south the approaches are bad, with both the path in Glen Nevis above Steall and also that up the Amhainn Rath from Loch Treighead poor and difficult to follow.

The hills offer more opportunities for snow-work than for rock-climbing, as, with the exception of the northern rock-face of Caisteal and the craggy southern corner of Sgùrr Innse, the sides of the ridges are mostly no more than steep slopes. In spring, however, the western group offers the opportunity of a magnificent ridge-walk, usually taken from north-east to south-west and started either up Coire na Gaibhre to the ridge of Stob Choire Claurigh or over the north-eastern top, Stob Coire na Ceannain. From the latter the ridge is narrow to the north top of Stob Choire Claurigh, after which it widens out and winds onward from one summit to another in a decidedly commonplace manner, although the descent from Stob Coire an Easain is rather rocky and broken up. The main features are the magnificent views of the Aonachs and Ben Nevis.

If the complete 5-mile course of the main ridge be followed, three 'Munros' – **Stob Choire Claurigh** (3858 ft.), **Stob Coire an Laoigh** (3659 ft.) and **Sgùrr Chòinnich Mòr** (3603 ft.) – and seven tops are included. This, however, leaves one far from one's starting point, with the easiest finish to the day a descent to Steall and Glen Nevis. A shorter variation is to leave the ridge at Stob Coire an Easain and go north to Beinn na Socaich – which has a claim to being a top in its own right – and thence down the beautiful Cour glen to Spean Bridge. A path will be found coming down from Coire Choimhlidh and crossing the Cour before the junction of the latter with the Allt an Loin, while a helpful finish is available in the motorable 2 miles from Leanachan Farm to the main road 1 mile west of Spean Bridge.

Stob Bàn (3217 ft.), standing on its own 1 mile S. by E. of Stob Choire Claurigh, is a shapely little peak with a steep finish. It may be climbed pleasantly from the end of the track through the Lairig

Leacach, or else worked into any one of several expeditions possible from Loch Treig-head.

The eastern group of the Grey Corries consists of the double-topped mountain whose south peak is **Stob Coire Easain** (3658 ft.), the culminating point, and whose north peak is **Stob a' Choire Mheadhoin** (3610 ft.). The main ridge runs N.N.E. from near Loch Treig-head and is bounded on the east by Loch Treig and on the west by the Lairig Leacach. Meall Cian Dearg is the north-eastern spur which overlooks Tulloch and provides the usual route to the higher summits farther south. **Sgùrr Innse** (2600 ft.) is a remarkable-looking hill, very steep on all sides. It rises precipitously for 1000 ft. above the summit of the Lairig Leacach and would appear to offer some scope for rock-scrambling, if nothing better. The easiest route will be found on the northern slopes, which are less rocky than the others. **Cruach Innse** (2800 ft.), just over a mile north-west of Sgùrr Innse, is bulkier and less formidably defended, its ridge forming the eastern flank of the pass.

The route from Glen Spean to the main summits of the eastern group is past Inverlair, either by way of the track which follows the west bank of the Allt Làire to a footbridge at 1000 ft., or by the Loch Treig dam. Thereafter the ridge of Meall Cian Dearg leads to Stob a' Choire Mheadhoin and, after a dip of 600 ft., to the fine summit of Stob Coire Easain, on which will be found a well-made cairn. The north-west corrie between the two peaks is fairly steep and usually holds a good depth of snow, useful for glissading to the Allt Làire on a descent from the bealach.

From Loch Treig-head it is probably easiest to start right up the slopes from the loch, leaving Creagan a' Chase on the right and climbing the long southern shoulder, Irlick Chaoile, to the summit of Stob Coire Easain.

BIBLIOGRAPHY

Scottish Mountains on Ski, Malcolm Slesser.
  (West Col, 1970.)

14

Rannoch Moor and Corrour

---

(1) *Stob Coire Sgriodain, North Top (3211 ft.). ¾ mile east of Loch Treig.
(2)   Stob Coire Sgriodain, South Top (3132 ft.). ⅓ mile S.S.E. of (1).
(3) *Chno Dearg (3433 ft.). 2 miles east of Loch Treig.
(4)   Meall Garbh (3197 ft.). Shoulder ¾ mile S.W. by W. of (3).
(5) *Beinn na Lap (3066 ft.). 1 mile north-west of Loch Ossian.
(6) *Beinn Eibhinn (3611 ft.). 3 miles W. by N. of Ben Alder.
(7)   Mullach Coire nan Nead (3025 ft.). 1 mile west of (6).
(8)   Uinneag a' Ghlas Choire (3041 ft.). ¾ mile W.S.W. of (6).
(9)   Beinn Chumhainn (2958 ft.). 2¼ miles W. by S. of Ben Alder.
(10) Sgòr Choinnich (3040 ft.). ⅝ mile north of (11).
(11) *Sgòr Gaibhre (3128 ft.). Between Loch Ossian and Loch Ericht.
(12) *Càrn Dearg (3084ft.). 3¾ miles east of Corrour Station.

The bleak expanse of Rannoch Muir – known of old as 'that thorofare of thieves' – has an area of some 56 square miles. Roughly triangular in shape, it is bounded on the west by the Black Mount and the old Glencoe road, on the north by the line of the Black Corries, and on the south-east by the Achaladair group and the high ground that continues to Loch Rannoch.

From Loch Tulla (540 ft.) the Moor rises in various places to over 1600 ft., the highest point being 1795 ft., yet so level is much of it that one could walk in a straight line for 10 miles between the 950 and 1000-ft. contours.

In glacial times the Moor was ice-covered and fed by glaciers that streamed down from the ice-caps of the surrounding heights. From it in turn the ice would spill over along what are now the main drainage-lines. At the north-west and south-west corners the river-flow is to the Atlantic by way of the Etive and the Orchy. It is, however, eastwards that the main drainage runs, the innumerable burns which rise in the heart of the Black Mount uniting to form the River Bà – 'river of cattle', doubtless from the old droving days. From the fastnesses of Corrie Bà, the latter crosses two miles of moorland, cuts below the old Glencoe road through a miniature gorge of red granite slabs, then flows in sluggish, picturesque curves to the island-studded network of Lochan na Stainge and Loch Bà. Thence the Abhainn Bà, Loch Laidon, the River Gaur, Loch Rannoch, the Tummel and the Tay continue the long, fascinating sequence to the North Sea.

After the ending of the Ice Age the Moor would be extensively wooded, and surviving fragments of the old pine forest may be seen in the Black Wood of Crannach ('black' wood is the same as 'dark' wood, or pine as opposed to oak and birch) and fringing Loch Tulla. Recently the Forestry Commission have re-planted an area beside the main road north of Loch Bà and another near Rannoch Station.

There is yet another, particularly fascinating side to the story of the Moor – the problem it presented during the construction of the West Highland Railway. Even before work on the latter began, a reconnaissance of the route, carried out by seven men in the depths of winter, was to become one of the legends of the line. The party left Spean Bridge by coach at daybreak on January 30, 1889, travelling to the north end of Loch Treig, whence they were rowed in an ancient boat to Creaguaineach Lodge at the head of the loch. Next day, in driving sleet, the men set out on their crossing, seemingly their most useful piece of equipment being an umbrella. Only one of the seven had had any previous experience of the Moor and it was not long before they were separated and in grave difficulties. It was only after an incredible struggle that they reached the southern fringe of the Moor, being extricated from their plight, surprisingly without casualty, by shepherds from Gorton cottage. Next day a severe blizzard broke over the West Highlands.

By June 1892 the new railway itself, starting from Craigendoran at one end and Fort William at the other, had reached the southern and northern edges of the Moor; in between was a gap – a morass of peat and heather – of nearly 20 miles. It was decided that the best solution would be to float the railway across the worst of the bog. First a vast drainage operation was carried out, then substantial foundations of turf and brushwood were laid, carrying soil and mountain till from the cuttings along the route and further augmented by thousands of tons of ash. North of Rannoch Station a depression had to be spanned by a viaduct of 684 ft., the longest on the line. Work during the following winter was slow, but a dry ensuing summer made amends and on September 5, 1893 the last length of rail was placed in position. In August of the next year the complete line was opened.

North-eastwards across the Moor the natural line of Loch Bà and

Loch Laidon forms to-day a tempting and worthwhile route for the canoeist or rubber dinghy enthusiast – particularly recommended by the light of a full moon. The crossing has also been made by skaters in the depths of a hard winter.

The track in the reverse direction, from Rannoch Station back to Kingshouse, begins well and also ends comfortably in four miles of actual road from Black Corries Lodge onwards; from Loch Laidon, however, past the ruined cottage of Tigh na Cruaiche, it is imaginary rather than real.

There are certainly many nowadays who have discovered in one way or another how wide of the mark Dr. John Macculloch was when he wrote of the Moor in 1811: 'It is indeed an inconceivable solitude; a dreary and joyless land of bogs, a land of desolation and grey darkness.'

From Rannoch Station the railway climbs gradually over 7 miles of the Moor to Corrour, the summit of the line at 1347 ft. A mile from here, at the west end of Loch Ossian, the youth hostel is a convenient centre for the neighbouring hills and starting-point for long cross-country expeditions, west to Glen Nevis or east to Dalwhinnie by way of the Bealach Dubh.

Stob Coire Sgriodain, North Top (3211 ft.), **South Top** (3132 ft.), **Chno Dearg** (3433 ft.) and **Meall Garbh** (3197 ft.) – These hills may be conveniently climbed in an 11-mile traverse from Corrour to Tulloch Station, or, of course, in the reverse direction with the addition of 600 ft. of ascent. They are mostly grass-covered and defended low down by tedious peat-hags. In good snow conditions, however, they are of interest to the skier, the traverse then making a really worth-while expedition.

From Corrour Station the way lies initially north-west along the Loch Treig path and from the hostel along the rather less boggy track which contours the lowest slopes of Beinn na Lap. These two paths converge where the Allt Luib Ruairidh comes in on the right. A slanting course north-eastwards up the long ridge, Garbh-bheinn, leads over Meall Garbh to Chno Dearg, the highest point of the group. A rather uninteresting tramp of $1\frac{1}{2}$ miles, with a drop of 500 ft., then leads round to the south top of Stob Coire Sgriodain, beyond which a further descent of 200 ft. and gradual rise up a broad ridge take one to the main, north top. From here the route is obvious down the north ridge to Tulloch.

On the east face of Meall Garbh a steep 500-ft. cliff of gneiss provides some interesting climbing. The quickest approach to this little-known area is to leave one's car at the Loch Treig dam and walk south up the railway for 1½ miles, then head directly over the shoulder of Stob Coire Sgriodain and through the gap between Chno Dearg and Meall Garbh; from this bealach it is only minutes to the foot of the crag. Total time from the dam: 2 hours. From Loch Ossian youth hostel it is probably better to take the longer way round by the loch road and Strath Ossian in preference to the very tedious approach by the Allt Luib Ruairidh and Allt Féith na h-Ealaidh.

The cliff, which is steeper than it looks from below, is split in the middle by an obvious diagonal gash. To the right or north of the latter is a deep, wet chimney which starts at the bottom of the cliff and converges with the gash at a prominent cave. Above this the gash continues to another, bigger cave, which appears from below to be near the top of the crag but is in fact only just over half way up. The gash has been climbed as far as the upper cave, but is wet, vegetatious and uninteresting apart from one tricky severe move at 80 ft. It should make a fine winter route.

Watcher's Wall. 250 ft. Severe. (P. N. L. Tranter and I. Rowe. October 1964.) Ascend the gash as far as the first cave or, preferably and more easily, traverse to this point from the left. Traverse right on a wet and slippery ledge till it would be possible to ascend easy, rotten terrain to the upper cave if this were desired. Instead, traverse further right by an obvious through-route to an easy ledge on the face, along which a deep-cut chimney is the start. Climb the chimney on loose rock for 80 ft. (D.) to a small, deep cave and chockstone belay; steep wall on right. Continue up line of chimney for 40 ft. to grass below an unclimbed groove (belay), close to the upper cave and the only obvious weakness on the wall. Climb a few feet up the groove then traverse horizontally right for 25 ft. (V.D.) to another chimney rising directly from the belay at the top of the first pitch. Climb this chimney for 20 ft. (M.S.), then keep left of an awkward central overhang, the crux (mild V.S.). In 10 ft. the climbing eases; peg belay on ledges above. This pitch is probably the easiest upward escape from the upper cave. Scrambling thereafter, with one short difficult pitch, leads to the top.

Hobson's Choice. 400 ft. Severe. (W. D. Fraser and A. R. M.

Park. October 1964.) Fifty yards left of the gash a grassy ledge slants up to the right. Follow this for 20 ft. and climb a split corner for 25 ft., using the right wall in the middle section. Trend leftwards to another obvious corner, also climbed initially on the right wall, then continue up grass to a belay at 100 ft. More grass and a large block lead to the buttress on the right (100 ft.). This soon steepens to the crux, near the nose of the ridge, above which easier rocks follow to the top.

Beinn na Lap (3066 ft.), belonging to the Forestry Commission and the Corrour Forest sanctuary, rises to the west of the deep trough of Strath Ossian, with Loch Ossian lying under its southern slopes. It has some crags on the eastern face, but is otherwise uninteresting. It is easily climbed from either end of Loch Ossian.

Beinn Eibhinn (3611 ft.), the highest point in the Forest, is only overtopped a few feet by its neighbour Aonach Beag, just across the march. The southern spurs are comparatively featureless, but the mountain presents a bold front to the north and falls almost from the summit cairn for 1000 ft. to the floor of Coire a' Chàrra Mhòir, a cirque of remarkable beauty and symmetry of form. Steep grassy slopes, strewn with granite blocks, drop for some 700 ft. to the cols which separate the summit ridge of Beinn Eibhinn from the subsidiary tops, **Mullach Coire nan Nead** (3025 ft.) and **Uinneag a' Ghlas Choire** (3041 ft.). On the floor of the saddle to the former are two curious lochans, lying close together, but at different levels and draining in opposite directions. The mountain finally terminates abruptly in the precipitous eastern wall of Strath Ossian, where crags of ice-worn granite form impressive portals to the glen. It is doubtful if these crags are anywhere of rock-climbing interest, although one reported possibility is a face some 250 ft. high on Creagan nan Nead, north-facing towards Loch Ghuilbinn.

Beinn Eibhinn is frequently climbed along with the hills in the group north of Ben Alder. From the west the best route is by the path from Corrour Lodge to the footbridge crossing the Uisge Labhair near where there is a good camping-site, then north up the long ridge overlooking Strath Ossian to Mullach Coire nan Nead, from which the cairn of Beinn Eibhinn lies 1 mile due east. Alternatively one can keep to the path, which continues for a further 3 miles along the right bank of the river until it disappears in the moorland opposite the Bealach Cumhann. Just over a mile from the bridge one can turn north up on to the ridge leading to Uinneag a' Ghlas Choire. The view from Beinn Eibhinn, especially of Creag Meagh-aidh and the western limits of the Monadh Liath, is very fine.

Beinn Chumhainn (2958 ft.) – The remaining hills of this group are the highest distinct tops of the long ridge which runs south-west and south from the western side of the Ben Alder massif, forming at once the march between the counties of Perth and Inverness and a part of the main watershed of Scotland. The summits and western spurs are smooth and for the most part carpeted with crisp fringe-moss and alpine sedge, delightful to walk upon. The Perthshire sides are, however, bold and rocky, and the granite slabs of Sgòr Choinnich and Sgòr Gaibhre and the long scarp of broken crags of schist over-looking the Allt Eigheach might repay exploration.

From Beinn Chumhainn, which presents a bold face to the north-east above the head of the Uisge Alder glen, the ridge runs for one mile south-west to Meall a' Bhealaich (2827 ft.), the intervening drop being about 400 ft. A further dip and a rise of 600 ft. then takes one in another mile to **Sgòr Choinnich** (3040 ft.), a fine steep hill with an impressive eastern corrie.

The ridge now trends due south for ¾ mile to the highest point, **Sgòr Gaibhre** (3128 ft.)crossing the Bealach nan Sgòr (2750 ft.) on the way. Thereafter the direction swings back to W.S.W., down to the Màm Bàn (2369 ft.) and up again to **Càrn Dearg** (3084 ft.)2 miles and about one hour from Sgòr Gaibhre.

The usual route to Sgòr Gaibhre from the Lodge is up the Allt a' Choire Chreagaich to its head and thence to the Bealach nan Sgòr. For Càrn Dearg the road from Corrour Station should be followed to the loch and then about 1½ miles farther east the moor should be crossed to the gradual western shoulder. Alternatively the remains of the Corrour Old Lodge track can be helpful for a short distance in making for this shoulder.

Càrn Dearg may also be approached from the south by way of the track which leaves the main road 1½ miles east of Rannoch Station – signposted 'Public Footpath to Fort William by Corrour (The Road to the Isles).' There is a locked gate at the start of this track, which is suitable for Land-Rovers only. To gain the Càrn Dearg ridge the Corrour Old Lodge path should be followed for some 2 miles beyond the junction of the Allt Eigheach and Allt Gormag, then the easiest line taken north-eastwards on to the long nose of Sròn Leachd a' Chaorruinn. The eastern crags of the ridge may also be reached from the junction of the two burns, with the help of a rough track which follows the Allt Eigheach for about $2\frac{1}{2}$ miles, while yet another alternative is to head north-eastwards after $\frac{3}{4}$ mile to the tops of Beinn Pharlagain (2836 ft.), the end of the $3\frac{1}{2}$-mile switchback running south from Sgòr Gaibhre.

BIBLIOGRAPHY

The West Highland Railway, John Thomas. (David and Charles, Newton Abbot. 1965.)

Undiscovered Scotland, W. H. Murray. (Dent. 1951.)

Always a Little Further, Alastair Borthwick. (John Smith, Glasgow. 1969.)

15

Ben Alder Group

(1) ***Ben Alder** (3757 ft.). On the west side of Loch Ericht, $11\frac{1}{2}$ miles from Dalwhinnie and 9 miles from Corrour Station.
(2) ***Beinn Bheòil** (3333 ft.). $1\frac{1}{4}$ miles east of (1).
(3)   **Sròn Coire na h-Iolaire** (3128 ft.). $\frac{3}{4}$ mile S.S.W. of (2).
(4)   **The Fara** (2986 ft.). $2\frac{1}{4}$ miles W.S.W. of Dalwhinnie Station.
(5) ***Aonach Beag** (3646 ft.). $2\frac{3}{4}$ miles W.N.W. of (1).
(6) ***Geal-Chàrn** (3688 ft.). 1 mile E.N.E. of (5).
(7)   **Sgòr Iutharn** (3300 ft.). 1 mile east of (6).
(8) ***Càrn Dearg** (3391 ft.). $2\frac{1}{4}$ miles north-east of (6).
(9)   **Diollaid a' Chàirn** (3029 ft.). $1\frac{1}{4}$ miles W.S.W. of (8).
(10) ***Beinn a' Chlachair** (3569 ft.). 4 miles N.N.W. of (1).
(11) ***Creag Pitridh** (3031 ft.). 6 miles north of (1).
(12) ***Mullach Coire an Iubhair** (3443 ft.). 1 mile east of (11).
(13)   **Sròn Garbh** (3320 ft.). $\frac{1}{2}$ mile E.S.E. of (12).

This magnificent group of mountains lies in the very heart of the Central Highlands, between the straight 14-mile stretch of Loch Ericht on the east and Loch Laggan on the north, and dropping south-westwards to the bleak expanse of Rannoch Moor.

The group falls naturally into three divisions: in the south Ben Alder proper, in the middle the great ridge running from Aonach Beag to Càrn Dearg, and in the north Beinn a' Chlachair and the other hills of the Ardverikie Forest.

The high, level plateau of Ben Alder itself, containing as it does no less than 380–400 acres of ground over 3500 ft., is a familiar feature in innumerable distant mountain views and catches the eye as surely as many more dramatically sculptured peaks. It is a granite-capped mountain, the lower slopes being composed of the schistose rocks, chiefly gneiss, characteristic of the Central Highlands. On the east the plateau falls away in steep, rough corries – the Gabhacorries – to Loch a' Bhealaich Bheithe, beyond which lies the ridge of Sròn Coire na h-Iolaire and Beinn Bheòil; on the north, towards the Bealach Dubh and the headwaters of the Culrea, it is fringed by a line of cliffs some 400–500 ft. high, while to the west and south-west it slopes away easily towards the Uisge Alder.

Ben Alder is not an easy mountain to reach, with long approach-marches necessary from whichever direction is chosen.

From the west the path to the Bealach Dubh from Corrour Station

27. Alder Bay, Loch Ericht. The view from what may have been the site of 'Cluny's Cage'.

and the Loch Ossian youth hostel becomes sketchy in places as it follows up the Uisge Labhair and finally disappears for good opposite the Bealach Cumhann. This certainly makes a long approach-route to Ben Alder and it should be treated with very considerable respect when the days are short and the weather is treacherous.

From the north the approach may be slightly shortened if permission can be obtained to use the Forestry Commission road to Strathossian Lodge (G.R. NN 405734). Alternative starting-points for this are on the Loch Laggan road ¾ mile west of Moy Lodge (good camping near Luiblea in a pleasant pinewood setting) or at Fersit, on the River Treig. From Strathossian Lodge continue south to Corrour Lodge and the approach up the Uisge Labhair.

From the north-east there is a road from Dalwhinnie down Loch Ericht to Ben Alder Lodge. This, although used regularly by the post van, is private and in addition is rough and frequently impassable owing to landslides. If permission is obtained, however, it may be possible to reach the ruined garage just short of Loch Pattack, where the car can be left and a way made south-westwards on foot to Culra Lodge, 2 miles farther on along the path to the Bealach Dubh. Good bothy accommodation may be had at Culra, the best centre for this side of the mountain.

From Culra to the summit of the Bealach Dubh (2300 ft.), between Ben Alder and Geal-Chàrn, is 3½ miles, the path circling thereafter round the western slopes of Ben Alder, crossing the Bealach Cumhann and descending the Alder Burn to Benalder Cottage on Loch Ericht.

The huge messy north-west face overlooking the Bealach Dubh was explored in February 1970 by R. N. Campbell and A. W. Ewing and found to have promising scope for long middle-grade winter routes and some harder possibilities. Approaching the cliffs from the north, a route was made up the first big buttress, mixed climbing (Grade II–III) leading to a little pot corrie with easy exit right.

An easy way to the plateau may be followed by leaving the path ¾ mile east of the saddle. Here a southerly course should be made up the burn which comes down from a steep little corrie, the summit plateau being reached about ¾ mile north of the cairn.

In addition to the path from Loch Pattack and Culra to the Bealach Dubh is one on the south bank of the Allt a' Chaoil-reidhe leading up to and along the east side of Loch a' Bhealaich Bheithe. From the moor between these two paths two long, narrow ridges rise to the summit plateau. The more northerly of these, the Long Leachas, gives a picturesque and pleasant scramble, at one point slightly exposed and vegetatious, and is the most direct route of ascent. The shorter ridge, about ½ mile south and forming the other arm of a fine corrie, Coire na Leith-chais, also gives an easy scramble and is known as the Short Leachas.

The Loch a' Bhealaich Bheithe path terminates about ½ mile beyond the south end of the loch and 300 ft. above it. This path is the usual route to Ben Alder from Dalwhinnie. The eastern slopes of Ben Alder, which overlook the loch and the path, are very steep, but only in places are they rocky and under good conditions may be ascended almost anywhere.

The prominent South Buttress of the Garbh Choire consists of a somewhat broken 1000-ft. mass on the left and, extending rightwards from the lower portion of this, a 300-ft. wall. The wall, which is continuous and fairly sound, is split centrally by two chimneys, the more prominent, right-hand of which has given a climb.

Uncle's Chimney. 300 ft. Very difficult. (A. R. M. Park, W. D. Fraser and P. N. L. Tranter. July 1962.) Climbed in three pitches, each 100 ft. First pitch partly on the right wall; second, involving an awkward chockstone, up the middle; third the hardest, again partly on the right wall. There are good belays, the rock is sound after the first 30 ft., and the standard is sustained throughout.

Undoubtedly the best 'advance' base for exploration is Benalder Cottage, superbly situated on Alder Bay, with pinewoods fringing the loch-side not far away. Sometimes bay and cottage are approached by canoe, but in planning for this it is perhaps worth remembering the loch's considerable length, 14 miles, and the fact that its steep-sided narrowness is apt to make it at times a hostile funnel for the wind. Apart from this and the approach by way of the Bealach Dubh, four routes to the cottage from the south-west may be mentioned, although again all are long and involve heavy cross-country work:

(1) Eastwards from Rannoch Station, then north-westwards along the Corrour Old Lodge track. Crossing the Allt Gormag, contour the south-eastern slopes of Beinn Pharlagain at 1250 ft. and cross the Cam Chriochan to Loch Ericht-side.

(2) Shorter, but as it necessitates the crossing of two large burns, only advisable if the weather is dry. From the Corrour Old Lodge track across the southern slopes of Sròn Smeur and to the right of Lochan Lòin nan Donnlaich to join the path running down to the bridge over the Cam Chriochan 100 yards from where the latter enters Loch Ericht.

(3) From the west end of Loch Rannoch, a good path round the west side of Meall Liath na Doire Mhòir to the Cam Chriochan bridge.

(4) From Bridge of Ericht on Loch Rannoch up the Hydro-Board road to the Ericht dam – the best of the four approaches, but permission for cars essential. From the dam the route goes north-west over very bad ground to the Cam Chriochan bridge, whence another $2\frac{1}{2}$ miles of rough going leads to the cottage.

From the cottage to the summit plateau, either the Bealach Breabag or Coire Chomhlain may be chosen. For those who favour skis the latter route – keeping parallel to the Alder Burn and some 400 yards above it – is recommended. From the cottage, too, a path, theoretical in places, leads back along the loch-side to Ben Alder Lodge.

Ben Alder was a familiar mountain as early as the 17th century, the name being given as 'Bin Aildir' by the famous mapmaker Blaeu. Alder itself has been said to mean 'rock water." High on the summit plateau is a lonely little lochan – Lochan a' Gharbh Choire – and Mr. Seton Gordon has commented that this, lying as it does at a height of some 3700 ft., must dispute with Lochan Buidhe on Ben Macdhui the claim to be the highest lochan in the Highlands.

Remoteness is probably Ben Alder's most attractive characteristic and it is hardly surprising that during his wanderings after Culloden, Prince Charlie found sanctuary among its isolated fastnesses. After spending nearly a fortnight at the eastern end of Loch Arkaig, the Prince had made his way into Badenoch travelling by the head of Glen Roy, over the ridge of Creag Meaghaidh and down to Ardverikie. Eventually, on August 30, 1746, he met Lochiel by the side of Loch Ericht, an event which called for some royal celebration – a hearty meal accompanied by 'an anker of whisky of twenty Scots pints'. Two or three days later they moved to the 'residence' of Cluny Macpherson, the celebrated 'Cluny's Cage', high on a spur of Ben Alder. This lonely shelter seems to have been remarkably commodious, for it was constructed against the sloping hillside, on two floors, out of wood and moss in a sea of great boulders. Well hidden by a thicket of holly, it afforded wide views, while the smoke of a fire merged into invisibility against its grey rock background. Here, in relative comfort, the Prince and his friends remained for a week, until news of the arrival of the French ships at Loch nan Uamh set him once more and finally on the move westwards. Unfortunately the exact site of the 'Cage' is now uncertain, although it is said to have been in the steep ground overlooking Loch Ericht, in the corrie north-east of Alder Bay.

Ardverikie, on the south shore of Loch Laggan, also has royal associations. King Fergus and four other early kings are said to be buried in what is now the garden, while Queen Victoria's fancy was greatly taken by the mansion in its beautiful loch-side setting of silver fir, spruce and pine, before the purchase of Balmoral. 'It is quite close to the lake,' she wrote in her *Journal*, 'and the view from the windows, as I now write, though obscured by rain, is very beautiful, and extremely wild. There is not a village, house, or cottage within four or five miles: one can only get to it by the ferry, or by rowing across the lake. The house is a comfortable shooting-lodge, built of stone, with many nice rooms in it. Stags' horns are placed along the outside and in the passages; and the walls of the drawing-room and ante-room are ornamented with beautiful drawings of stags, by Landseer.'

Sròn Coire na h-Iolaire (3128 ft.) and **Beinn Bheòil** (3333 ft.). From the summit of Ben Alder the descent to the Bealach Breabag (2700 ft.) lies first south-west and then south-east, altogether 1 mile. The col forms a delightful resting-place on short springy turf, with fine views down to Alder Bay and the south end of Loch Ericht. Thereafter it is a climb of just over 400 ft. to the distinct top of the Sròn and almost another mile to Beinn Bheòil along the long regular ridge, very steep screes dropping away on the one hand to Loch a' Bhealaich Bheithe and grassier slopes on the other as steeply to Loch Ericht.

The Fara (2986 ft.). The summit of The Fara lies only 2¼ miles W.S.W. of Dalwhinnie Station and from it a most enjoyable high-level walk of a further 2½ miles may be had to Meall Cruaidh (2941 ft.), with descent if so desired to Ben Alder Lodge. The views from this ridge are especially rewarding and certainly among the finest in the Dalwhinnie district: Loch Ericht seen throughout its entire length and Ben Alder, near at hand; farther off, Ben More, Ben Cruachan, the Glencoe and Mamore hills and Ben Nevis.

A mile north of the summit of The Fara and 3 miles W.N.W. of Dalwhinnie is a narrow defile, the Dirc Mhòr, over ½ mile long and described as resembling a miniature Llanberis Pass. The southern wall is lined with a number of small but impressive buttresses, sound micro-granite and feldspar.

Sentinel Rock – Holy Smoke. 300 ft. Very severe. (A. McKeith and party. August 1966.) On the biggest and most impressive buttress, lying at the Dalwhinnie end of the Dirc Mhòr. Start above and right of lowest rocks in the lowest of three grassy alcoves leading on to the buttress. Climb a short wall, then move right across a slab and up over two large blocks to a ledge. Climb wall above by crack on right to third grassy alcove (100 ft.). Climb a corner on left, then left again along ledge out on to the wall of the buttress and up to belay on small ledges on a slab (80 ft.). Up the left edge of the corner above to a prominent roof, left to a large block, then hand-traverse up and rightwards until a narrow ledge leads right. Go straight up then left to a slab and follow the crest to the top (120 ft.).

Aonach Beag (3646 ft.) is the most westerly summit of the great mountain plateau to the north of Ben Alder which rivals the latter in extent. Quite distinct ridges, reminiscent of the Mamores, run out from it to north-west and also S.S.W. to Beinn Eibhinn, from which it is often climbed, but eastwards the slopes fall gradually for 300 ft. before rising again to merge in the most extensive part of the plateau, **Geal-Chàrn** (3688 ft.). A considerable expanse of the latter lies above the 3500-ft. contour and when the huge snowfields there melt, stretches of pasture-land are left, providing excellent feeding ground for the deer. Just over a mile away, **Sgòr Iutharn** (3300 ft.) is the top of the well-known Lancet Edge, the narrow, rocky eastern ridge of the Geal-Chàrn plateau. It is not named on the one-inch O.S. map, but is shown by the small 3250-ft. contour. Coming from the Dalwhinnie direction along the path to the Bealach Dubh, the Edge is the obvious route to Geal-Chàrn. It soon steepens and becomes quite narrow, with rocky steps formed by the usual schistose outcrops. Except under snow conditions there is no difficulty, but care is necessary for several hundred feet – and especially on the descent. As the top is approached, the slope on the left to the Bealach Dubh becomes less steep, but precipitous rocks continue on the right overlooking Loch an Sgòir. Continuing east from the summit of Geal-Chàrn, an interesting section of ridge leads to the intervening top of **Diollaid a' Chàirn** (3029 ft.), an almost imperceptible rise, then on broader ground to the final summit of the plateau, **Càrn Dearg** (3391 ft.). From Loch Pattack the path running south to the Culrea Burn is helpful in an ascent of Càrn Dearg from the east.

For the remaining mountains in this group – those in the Ardverikie Forest – the estate road from the north-east end of Loch Laggan is the most convenient approach. This is strictly private, however, as

28. Grey Corries, Aonachs and Ben Nevis, from Loch Lochy.

is indicated at the entrance-bridge over the River Pattack, and locked gates farther in bar access by car both to Lochan na h-Earba and to Loch Pattack. Permission may nevertheless be granted and application should be made to the estate factor at Gallovie (G.R. NN 552891).

If a car is taken to Lochan na h-Earba with Creag Pitridh and Mullach Coire an Iubhair (Geal Chàrn on the one-inch O.S. map) in view, it should be left at the far end of the north-eastern portion of the loch, whence a very good stalking path climbs in a pleasant curve up the Allt a' Mhaigh to cross the bealach (2600 ft.) between the two hills. **Creag Pitridh** (3031 ft.) is a prominent little mountain with a well-defined west ridge but eastern slopes that fall away more gradually to the broad, boggy saddle. **Mullach Coire an Iubhair** (3443 ft.) is easy and unattractive-looking as seen from the col, although more imposing from the flat ground to the east. The slopes, which fall south-westwards from it and its subsidiary top, **Sròn Garbh** (3320 ft.), form one side of the high pass holding Loch a' Bhealaich Leamhain.

As well as being easily reached from the Creag Pitridh bealach, both Mullach and Sròn may be approached from the road running south beside the River Pattack (suitable for Land-Rovers only). Just over 1 mile short of Loch Pattack a path goes off to the west, crossing eventually to Lochan na h-Earba. Midway along this yet another branch turns up usefully into the corrie between the two tops.

Beinn a' Chlachair (3569 ft.) – lent character by the impressive north-facing cirque of Coire Mòr a' Chlachair – may be linked with the other summits in a not-too-long day. For this the path which runs from the south-west portion of Lochan na h-Earba over the Bealaich Leamhain to Loch Pattack will be found helpful. Alternatively its western slopes may be reached from the main Loch Laggan road ¾ mile west of Moy Lodge.

A recent rock-climbing discovery of growing popularity is Binnein Shuas, a 2400-ft. hill which presents a formidable face to Lochan na h-Earba. The usual approach to this is from the west, leaving the Loch Laggan road at the point just mentioned – ¾ mile west of Moy Lodge. A path on the right bank of the Amhainn Ghuilbinn leads to a fence which crosses the moor to an estate road and the latter is followed in turn to Lochan na h-Earba. The rocks are then a further 20 minutes distant, or altogether about 1¼ hours from the main road.

On approaching the crag, which is about 500 ft. high and composed mainly of micro-granite and feldspar, one is faced by a huge wall, the West Sector, with massive overhangs, The Fortress, at its right end. Behind the latter is Hidden Gully and beyond that again Ardverikie Wall on the East Sector. The routes, which were first described in detail in S.M.C.J. Vol. XXIX. No. 159, pp. 67–69, are given from left to right. The crag was first explored in the spring of 1964. Hidden Gully (or Gimcrack as it was then named) was climbed in April by C. S. M. Doake, J. Gilchrist and P. N. L. Tranter; in May, R. Ford, T. W. Patey and Mrs. M. Stewart did the top part of The Fortress and other minor climbs; then, in the summers of 1967 and 1968, D. F. Lang and G. N. Hunter made no less than eleven new routes, thus demonstrating the excellent potential of the cliff.

Blaeberry Grooves. 250 ft. Very severe. (D. F. Lang and G. N. Hunter. September 1967.) Lies up the imposing wall between the

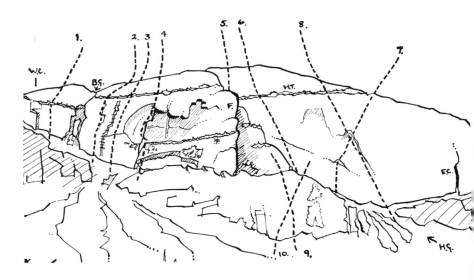

CLIFFS OF BINNEIN SHUAS

1. Blaeberry Grooves;   2. Cube Wall;   3. Kubla Khan;   4. The Keep;
5. Merrydown;   6. Flypaper;   7. Hairline Grooves;   8. Ardverikie Wall;
9. Cross;   10. Criss.

obvious watercourse to the left, West Chimney, and Broken Gully. Climb obvious crack in centre of face to ledge and thread belay (peg runner) (100 ft.). Gain slab above and follow central crack line easily to top (150 ft.).

Gorgon. 300 ft. Very severe. (J. Mackenzie and N. Fraser.) Crack to right of Blaeberry Grooves. Above, slabs lead to an awkward dièdre, a leftward traverse and easier slabs.

Cube Wall. 400 ft. Severe. (D. F. Lang and G. N. Hunter. September 1967.) From corner below a recent rockfall climb crack to ledge on left. Move left from quartz cube (peg), up to diagonal fault, thence into large corner and up to grass (110 ft.). Climb wall above to terrace (70 ft.). From boulder on right a short layback crack leads to easy groove crossing Kubla Khan and belay at quartz knob (130 ft.). Finish directly up slab.

Kubla Khan. 370 ft. Severe. (D. F. Lang and G. N. Hunter. June 1967.) On slabby wall left of The Fortress. Start to right of dyke at ledge below first wall left of overhangs. Climb steep grooved wall to juniper bush on large ledge (60 ft.), then grooved slab above until forced left onto small ledge with recess (150 ft.). Continue over terrace to overhang and lichenous slab above.

The Keep. 450 ft. Very severe. (D. F. Lang and G. N. Hunter. July 1967.) Follows left edge of The Fortress. Above rowan tree on grassy ramp climb outside of crack on left wall (40 ft.). Grooves on edge of buttress lead to two vertical cracks. Climb left-hand crack using 2 pegs and slings. From top peg enter right-hand crack to reach large flake; continue up this fault, passing loose block, to emerge on slab, then easily up to grass patch and belays (140 ft., crux, very exposed). Climb slab to terrace and belay in small cave (100 ft.), thence hogsback ridge on right to top.

The Fortress. 400 ft. Very severe. (R. Ford, T. W. Patey and Mrs. M. Stewart. May 1964.) The top part was climbed, approaching by the hanging garden on left. From a small triangular overhang, crack above roof was climbed for 20 ft., then a 10-ft. tension traverse made to edge on right which was followed to the top.

Hidden Gully. 450 ft. Very difficult. (C. S. M. Doake, J. Gilchrist and P. N. L. Tranter. April 1964.) A short chockstone pitch; 200 ft. of mixed difficult climbing; another chockstone, severe but well protected; thereafter scrambling. In winter Grade II, with numerous short ice pitches.

Merrydown. 170 ft. Severe. (D. F. Lang and G. N. Hunter. June 1967.) Start at junction of the terrace with Hidden Gully above the gully's crux. Climb rib, move right and up past small overhang to ledge and belay (70 ft.). Climb wall above then easy to top.

Flypaper. 370 ft. Very severe. (D. F. Lang and G. N. Hunter. June 1967.) Start at cairn in Hidden Gully about 200 ft. up where it begins to narrow. Climb steep red wall on small holds and continue over small overhang to birch tree in corner. Short of the tree go right to ledge and thread belay (130 ft.). Back horizontally left for 25 ft. (peg runner) then up 30 ft. and left to terrace (90 ft.). Climb prominent red streak above to flake runner. Leave flake on small holds to layback crack and follow to top.

Usquebaugh. 570 ft. Severe. (G. N. Hunter and D. F. Lang. June 1968.) Start at red waterworn streak 50 ft. below start of Hairline Grooves (cairn). Climb wall to grass ledge and by corner on left to peg belay above white scar (150 ft.). Follow staircase and rib to below overhang (140 ft.); surmount corner on left to grass ledge, slab and terrace (130 ft.); finish with short overhang, scoop and rib on left to final peg belay.

Hairline Grooves. 400 ft. Severe. (D. F. Lang and G. N. Hunter. September 1967.) Follow a thin crack across Ardverikie Wall. Start at obvious waterworn fault at the foot of Hidden Gully (cairn). Climb left of flake spike, move up and go right to a line of cracks which follow to black rocks and gravel ledge. Belay here or at prominent white scar above (90 ft.). Climb up from the right of the scar until a crack can be discerned and climb it up to and through an overlap to belay on third pitch of Ardverikie Wall (120 ft.). Step off belay flake and continue up faint crack to thread belay (130 ft.). East to terrace.

Ardverikie Wall. 550 ft. Severe. (D. F. Lang and G. N. Hunter. June 1967.) A classic route, one of the best of its standard – mild severe – in Scotland. Its appearance belies its grading and, with the exception of the first pitch and some lichen on the rib, it is on perfect rock throughout with magnificent situations. It takes a direct line up the centre of the main buttress. Start at the lowest rocks right of Hidden Gully and some 25 ft. left of a large boulder forming an arch (cairn). Climb rib then heather to belay in niche (40 ft.). Regain rib and climb it direct to slab. Trend right, then back left to ledge and flake belay (130 ft.). Up slab into scoop below overlap, climb overlap on large holds or move right to ledge, then up to flake belay (100 ft.). Move right from belay to holds (crux) then slightly left up ill-defined rib to belay below large scoop (125 ft.). Up and over small overlap to quartz vein, which follow to terrace (55 ft.). Finish up easy slabs (100 ft.).

Criss. 200 ft. Severe. (T. W. Patey, R. Ford and Mrs. M. Stewart. May 1964.) Climb rightward trending crack in two pitches to top.

Cross. 180 ft. Very severe. (T. W. Patey, R. Ford and Mrs. M. Stewart. May 1964.) Start at first fault right of Criss. Climb straight up then left crossing Criss and follow corner till it overlaps. Break through overlap and finish directly.

Differential. 200 ft. Very severe. (J. McDowell and D. Todd. May 1969.) Up the wall left of the detached block of Tip Top, on good varied rock, exposed and well protected. From turf-filled corner of Tip Top climb diagonally left past pocket of grass at 60 ft. until moves up slab lead to definite traverse left into obvious groove (peg runner). Climb groove and break awkwardly right to continue diagonally right past shelf overhang to belay. Go left till easy chimney leads to top.

Tip Top. 230 ft. Very severe. (J. McDowell and D. Todd. May 1969.) Some 50 yards from Eastern Chimney is a conspicuous detached block. Start at left end of block at broken corner. Climb corner to base of black, lichen-covered corner. Traverse right with difficulty onto edge of detached block. Continue up to grass ledge and belay (70 ft.). Climb obvious corner on right for 50 ft. till traverse right can be made along defined line to arête. Follow arête to belay on flat ledge (120 ft.). Climb crack and continue in quartz fault to top (40 ft.).

Second Prize. 240 ft. Severe. (J. Cunningham and C. Higgins. May 1969.) At right-hand end of face of East Sector are the East Chimneys. Climb left-hand chimney and short wall; move right into large slabby corner; surmount this and layback flake on left to belay on ledge (140 ft.). After another short corner cross broken ground to belay.

Eastern Chimney. 300 ft. Severe. (J. McDowell and D. Todd. May 1969.) The right-hand chimney, marked on diagram p. 142. Climb chimney to grass ledge (150 ft.). Continue in chimney, then break left and reach conspicuous corner. Climb this and rocks above to belay.

Soft Shoe Shuffle. 300 ft. Very severe. (G. N. Hunter and D. F. Lang. May 1968.) This route on the Far East Sector lies up the steep clean wall about 300 ft. right of Ardverikie Wall. Start at cairn on flat slab and surmount awkward overhang to reach flake. Traverse right to obvious crack and climb this to flake belay on ledge. Traverse left under overhang for 25 ft., break through overhang on large blocks and go up to peg belay on ledge. Climb corner on right then go diagonally right following line of flakes to flake belay and stance at 60 ft. Continue up obvious steep quartzband on left and climb directly, breaking through several overhangs on good holds to block belay at 130 ft. Easy climbing for 200 ft. leads to the terrace.

Whiplash. 150 ft. Very severe. (G. N. Hunter and D. F. Lang. May 1968.) On the lowest crag of the Far East Sector. An obvious series of grooves and a chimney split this short but clean wall. Start at cairn and ascend grooves to reach spike on left of overhanging chimney. Move up left to reach small sloping ledge. Climb corner above to good spike and traverse right under overhanging edge to gain the chimney (peg runner). Follow chimney to stance and peg belay. Climb steep left wall to reach small ledge and continue up right on small holds to thread belay at top.

16

Drumochter Hills

(1) ***Sgairneach Mhòr** (3210 ft.). 3 miles west of Dalnaspidal Station.
(2) ***Beinn Udlamain** (3306 ft.). 1 mile W. by N. of (1).
(3) ***A'Mharconaich** (3185 ft.). 2 miles north-east of (2).
(4) ***Geal Chàrn** (3005 ft.). 4½ miles S.S.W. of Dalwhinnie.
(5) **Stob an Aonaich Mhòir** (2805 ft.). 3¾ miles south-west of (2).
(6) **Meall na Leitreach** (2544 ft.). 2 miles south of Dalnaspidal Station.
(7) **Beinn Mholach** (2758 ft.). 6 miles south-west of Dalnaspidal Station.
(8) **Beinn a' Chuallaich** (2925 ft.). 2½ miles N.N.E. of Kinloch Rannoch.

This group is enclosed in the large triangle, the apex of which is Dalwhinnie and the base the valley of Loch Rannoch and Loch Tummel. Loch Ericht, lying south-west to north-east, forms one side, while the other is the irregular line of road and railway climbing from Blair Atholl over Drumochter.

Sgairneach Mhòr, Beinn Udlamain, and A'Mharconaich form a horseshoe round the grassy Coire Dhomhain, with Geal Chàrn as an outlier to the north. Smooth-topped and with no big intervening drops, all four summits can be traversed in one expedition without undue difficulty. These are hills especially interesting to the skier, perhaps less well known in this respect than those on the east side of the road and railway, but under good conditions considerably more rewarding.

To those crossing Drumochter the group is familiar also as including the conspicuous Boar of Badenoch, or An Torc (2422 ft.), immediately west of the summit level at the county march, and the Sow of Atholl (2500 ft.), 1½ miles farther south.

Sgairneach Mhòr (3210 ft.) – From Dalnaspidal Station the route lies south-west past the cottages to the bridge over the Allt Dubhaig, and then up the Allt Coire Luidhearnaidh, keeping to the left bank until a north-west course leads up easy slopes to the top. The point marked 3160 on the one-inch map is ⅓ mile south-west of the highest point, which is on the broad ridge running roughly east and west and is marked by a small cairn. The summit appears to be at least 100 ft. higher than the 3160-ft. top. The northern slopes are fringed by a range of cliffs about 300 ft. high overlooking Coire Creagach. There is also a good route up the Allt Coire Dhomhain by a path on the left bank reached from the main road 1½ miles north of Dalnaspidal Station. From the minor summit (3160 ft.) an excellent ski run goes down the course of the burn running due north into the Dhomhain valley, where it joins the path referred to above.

From Sgairneach Mhòr to the Sow of Atholl the route lies at first down the fairly well-defined ridge to the east and north-east, then on broader slopes at the bealach and for the re-ascent. The highest point of the Sow is near the north end of the 2500-ft. contour. A descent can be made down the easy south-east ridge and a direct line taken to Dalnaspidal Station if the river is low, or to the bridge in times of flood.

To continue from Sgairneach Mhòr to **Beinn Udlamain** (3306 ft.) is not quite simple in misty weather. It is best to go south-west for 600 yards and then north-west for 800 yards to the top marked 3053 ft., whence a descent of 400 ft. and ½ mile, again south-west, places one on the saddle. Beinn Udlamain is then reached by its south ridge.

From Udlamain the ridge runs N.N.E. for ½ mile to an unnamed 3213-ft. top, then north-east, dropping only to 2800 ft., to the great broad plateau of **A'Mharconaich** (3185 ft.). There are fine views from this ridge, although skiers may find its exposure in windy weather makes it prone to sheet ice. On A'Mharconaich a height of 3174 ft. is reached on the county boundary (fence), but the actual summit is ½ mile away, near the N.N.E. corner of the 3150-ft. contour. There are three smallish cairns fairly close together, of which the most westerly appears to mark the highest point. From the summit plateau an excellent ski run is often to be had down into Coire Fhàr, continuous in good conditions right back to the road.

The Boar of Badenoch is easily climbed if one is returning to the Drumochter Pass, its north and north-east slopes being steep and the simplest way down by the south-east. Otherwise A'Mharconaich's north-east ridge – usually characterised high up in winter and spring by an impressively large cornice – may be followed pleasantly down for 2¼ miles to the bridge just short of Drumochter Lodge.

Geal Chàrn (3005 ft.) – From the bridge a well-marked track cuts across the flank of Geal Chàrn and runs right up to the bealach with A'Mharconaich. This makes a useful start when climbing Geal Chàrn itself, a line then being taken on to the latter's broad east ridge. The three cairns or butts on the ridge, so clearly seen from the valley, may in mist or winter white-out be mistaken for the summit. In fact they lie at about 2750 ft., and the top of the mountain, marked by a single cairn, is just over ½ mile due west from the highest of the butts. The bealach between the S.S.W. ridge of Geal Chàrn and the undulating grassy slopes climbing again south-eastwards to A'Mharconaich is 2426 ft.

Stob an Aonaich Mhòir (2805 ft.) is remotely situated on Loch Ericht-side directly opposite Ben Alder. From Bridge of Ericht, on Loch Rannoch, a Hydro-Electric Board road runs for 3½ miles to the dam at the foot of Loch Ericht and makes a helpful approach. This, however, is private and the proprietor has stated that no vehicles are allowed on it. The address of the head stalker is Tighness, Killichonan. *Meall na Leitreach* (2544 ft.) overlooks Loch Garry directly south of Dalnaspidal, while **Beinn Mholach** (2758 ft.), highest point of the moorland to the south-west, is more easily reached from Loch Rannoch, a rough private road climbing 5½ miles from Craiganour Lodge, where permission to use a car may be obtained. **Beinn a' Chuallaich** (2925 ft.) is Schichallion's counterpart on the north side of the Tummel valley, a long ridge running up easily to the summit from the Dunalastair Reservoir and probably making a more pleasant approach than the steeper, shorter climb from the hill road over to Trinafour.

17

Glen Roy to Creag Meaghaidh

(1) **Beinn Iaruinn** (2636 ft.). 5¾ miles N. by E. of Roy Bridge Station.
(2) **Càrn Dearg** (2677 ft.). 3 miles E.S.E. of south end of Loch Oich.
(3) **Càrn Dearg** (2523 ft.). 1¼ miles S.S.E. of (2).
(4) **Càrn Dearg, Glen Roy** (2736 ft.). 5¼ miles N. by W. of Tulloch Station.
(5) **Beinn Teallach** (2994 ft.). 3½ miles north of Tulloch Station.
(6) ***Beinn a' Chaoruinn (South Top)** (3437 ft.). 3¼ miles N.N.E. of Tulloch Station.
(7) **Beinn a' Chaoruinn (North Top)** (3422 ft.). ¾ mile N. by W. of (6).
(8) ***Creag Meaghaidh** (3700 ft.). 2½ miles north-east of (6).
(9) **An Cearcallach** (3250 ft.). 1⅛ miles S. by E. of (8).
(10) **Meall Coire Choille-rais** (3299 ft.). 1 mile south-east of (8).
(11) **Puist Coire Ardair** (3591 ft.). 1 mile east of (8).
(12) **Creag Mhòr** (3496 ft.). 1½ miles east of (8).
(13) ***Poite Coire Ardair** (3460 ft.). 1 mile north-east of (8).
(14) **Poite Coire Ardair (East Top)** (3441 ft.). ½ mile E.N.E. of (13).
(15) **Sròn Garbh Choire** (3250 ft.). 1⅜ miles E.N.E. of (13).
(16) **Meall an t-Snaim** (3180 ft). 1 mile north-east of (15).
(17) ***Càrn Liath** (3298 ft.). 3½ miles west of Loch Laggan Hotel.
(18) **A'Bhuidheanach** (3177 ft.). ½ mile E.N.E. of (17).
(19) **Stob Choire Dhuibh** (3002 ft.). 1¾ miles north-east of (17).

There must be few parts of Inverness-shire of comparable size less well known than that vast, desolate triangle with its base Glen Spean and Loch Laggan and its apex Fort Augustus. Innumerable motorists, of course, are familiar with the Spean Bridge-Newtonmore road and even more with the A82 along Loch Lochy and Loch Oich; relatively often too the third side, the Corrieyairack Pass, has its visitors. But the hinterland behind the thick curtain of the Great Glen woods, beyond the barrier edge of Creag Meaghaidh – the lonely hills round the headwaters of the Turret and the Roy, or remote moorland lochs like Loch Spey and Loch Roy – is left for the most part in uninterrupted peace.

One corner, however, which deservedly is becoming better known is Glen Roy. Up it for 8½ miles a well-surfaced road – single-track with passing-places – twists and climbs to Turret Bridge at 800 ft.

(a venture, incidentally, to be undertaken with a good deal of circumspection under conditions of snow or ice). In its earlier stages the road cuts across the side of a steep, pleasantly wooded hill-slope high above the river. Opposite, the moors gradually bend back and open out to give glimpses of **Beinn Teallach** (2994 ft.) four miles away at the head of Gleann Glas Dhoire.

Three miles up from Roy Bridge, on the flank of Bohuntine Hill and opposite the point at which the Allt Uilleim joins the Roy, a spacious parking-place has been provided. From here superb views are to be had back to the Aonachs and Grey Corries, and also of the Parallel Roads, now partly included in an area which was declared a national nature reserve in 1970. Beyond the deserted croft of Achavady the glen becomes more open, with the road and river approaching each other more closely.

The road crosses the flank of **Beinn Iaruinn** (2636 ft.), with its distinctive Coire nan Eun, while **Càrn Dearg** (2736 ft.) almost opposite would be just as easily reachable. Beyond Turret Bridge the road deteriorates and eventually becomes a path over the col (1151 ft.) to Melgarve, 9 miles away on the track to the Corrie-yairack. For **Càrn Dearg** (2677 ft.) and **Càrn Dearg** (2523 ft.), $1\frac{1}{4}$ miles apart, the most obvious route is to take the path up Glen Turret then climb out on to the moors by way of the Allt Eachach.

The phenomena of the Parallel Roads of Glen Roy, which have for long been of great interest to geologists and which in fact occur in Glen Spean and Glen Gloy as well as in Glen Roy, are classic examples of terraces formed along the shores of an ice-drained lake. Ice extending northwards from the Ben Nevis area blocked the mouths of Glen Roy and Glen Gloy, and behind this barrier the lake formed. The Roads are found at three levels which average 1148 ft., 1067 ft., and 855 ft. These levels represent successive stages of the lowering of the lake, determined by the uncovering, as the ice barrier retreated, of lower cols which provided outlets for the water. In Glen Roy all three levels are present, while in Glen Gloy only the highest, at 1165 ft., is found, and in Glen Spean only the lowest, at 855 ft.

The more important hills of the group, from Beinn a' Chaoruinn to the eastern neighbours of Creag Meaghaidh, are very much better known than the remote summits of Glen Roy. The road along Loch Laggan-side becomes busier with visitors every summer, while Coire Ardair has at last indisputably come into its own as one of the finest winter climbing areas in Britain.

29. Beinn a' Chaoruinn, East Face.

Looking across Loch Laggan to the magnificent pines and spruces of Ardverikie, one is apt to forget how much of the north side also is pleasantly wooded – deciduous trees clustered round innumerable shingle bays, then towards the south-west end of the loch, dense screens of conifers. Off Ardverikie mansion itself the two islets in the loch have associations with the ancient kings of Scotland: on Eilean an Righ, 'the king's isle', King Fergus is said to have had his hunting lodge; on Eilean nan Con, 'the island of the hounds', the dogs were kept.

The artificial extension to Loch Laggan, formerly 4 miles of the River Spean from Lublea to beyond Roughburn, is less picturesque and consequently less attractive, almost as though resentful of the spoliation caused by the building of the dam at the western end. Bleak, rather featureless moorland to north and south of the valley does nothing to make amends.

Beinn a' Chaoruinn (3437 ft.) is easily ascended by way of its southern slopes from Glen Spean, either from the Laggan dam or from Craigbeg, 2 miles farther east. The backbone of the mountain itself is a long, gently undulating ridge leading from the main summit to the subsidiary northern top (3422 ft.). It passes over a slight rise mid-way – a top of 3394 ft. given a place originally in Munro's Tables – and to this latter a narrow ridge rises steeply from the floor of Coire na h-Uamha, providing an interesting and relatively easy route of ascent. This ridge is conspicuous from the corrie and has a pinnacle near its foot.

At the head of Coire na h-Uamha the high ground connecting Beinn a' Chaoruinn with Creag Meaghaidh drops at its lowest point to the Bealach a' Bharnish (2686 ft.).

In 1746, during the final days of his flight, Prince Charlie and his friends surmounted the barrier of the Creag Meaghaidh range, although it is not known if they actually went out of their way to 'bag' any tops. Creag Meaghaidh, however, seems to have been climbed in July 1819 by the energetic Ordnance Survey engineer Major-General Colby and some of his men in the course of their mountain exploration of the Highlands.

Creag Meaghaidh (3700 ft.) – The extensive summit plateau, roughly one square mile of it lying above 3250 ft., slopes gently to the south, although to the north there is a line of steep ground and precipices. Near the edge of the latter, about 400 yards north-east of the summit, is a gigantic cairn said to have been erected by a madman in memory of his wife. Five hundred feet below is Lochan Uaine, which drains into the Roy, while 1 mile east are the magnificent cliffs of Coire Ardair. To the south and east the plateau runs out into three ridges culminating in the subsidiary tops of An Cearcallach, Meall Coire Choille-rais and Creag Mhòr. The view from the summit is not particularly good, although the Parallel Roads of Glen Roy are well seen and Ben Nevis and the Aonachs show up well towards the south-west.

From Craigbeg in Glen Spean, a long but gentle ascent, mostly over grass, provides an easy though rather dull way up. More interesting is to make a round of all the tops, choosing a starting-point on Loch Laggan-side mid-way between Aberardair Farm and Moy Lodge. **Creag Mhòr** (3496 ft.) and **Puist Coire Ardair** (3591 ft.) can be visited on the way to the summit, with impressive views into the cirque of Coire Ardair on the one hand and on the other of the fine corrie with its lochan and 700-ft. cliffs between **Meall Coire Choille-rais** (3299 ft.) and Creag Mhòr. The descent takes in the final top, **An Cearcallach** (3250 ft.), before dropping steeply to the moor again and eventually the main road at the west end of the woods.

Creag Meaghaidh – Coire Ardair (*a description by A. McKeith*)

Coire Ardair, on the eastern flank of Creag Meaghaidh, is one of the largest and most impressive corries in Scotland, its cliffs second only to those of Ben Nevis for both scale and grandeur. In contrast to Nevis, however, the rock-climbing potential is limited. The rock, a horizontally stratified mica-schist, is for the most part badly frost-shattered and supports a heavy growth of vegetation. Existing rock-climbs, which follow most of the more obvious buttresses and gullies, are remarkable only for length and situation, although with an eye to the future it is conceivable that some of the large clean walls which are to be found may provide good modern rock-climbs of a high standard.

Coire Ardair is essentially a winter corrie. Its rocks usually hold plenty of snow and the majority of routes will, at some time or other, be in condition. It is probably the most accessible winter cliff of its size in Britain, and since it is centrally placed in Scotland, the worst weather of both east and west coasts is avoided.

The corrie is less than 4 miles from Aberardair Farm, so that most of the climbs can be reached relatively easily in 2 hours. The cliffs are not visible from the farm as the valley leading up to the corrie is L-shaped. The best approach is by a good path high on the right side of the glen, first north then west. The path continues diagonally right up to the Window, but in winter it is usually completely obliterated higher up. For this reason one should descend to another path in the valley floor about 1 mile before reaching the lochan, as this then becomes the best approach to the majority of the routes. The routes on Belleview Buttress may also be approached directly up the ridge from Aberardair Farm, but this is recommended only if one is certain that the correct way is known. Again, if the ridge is clear of mist, or if the way is known, this makes the best descent from all the routes, otherwise one may descend either by Easy Gully or by the Window.

To date Coire Ardair harbours some 36 winter climbs, a number of which must have an undisputed claim to rank amongst the finest undertakings in the British Isles, most certainly in the class of those on Ben Nevis and Lochnagar. The cliffs, which are over $1\frac{1}{2}$ miles long, face north-east and reach a maximum height of 1500 ft. They are divided into four main sections: from left to right, Belleview Buttress, Pinnacle Buttress (one of the most imposing single features of any British corrie), the Post Face, and the Inner Coire. Each of these provides a number of climbs, all of which are good given the right conditions, while a select few bear particular mention. In the following brief descriptions measurements throughout are by rope lengths.

Belleview Buttress – the large buttress on the left side of the corrie – is defined on its right edge by a prominent right-angled corner, *Eastern Corner* (1000 ft.; Grade III). This was first climbed by M. Slesser and K. Bryan in 1961 and has since proved fairly popular. *Raeburn's Gully* (1200 ft.; Grade II) is the next obvious gully, slanting up leftwards to the plateau under the imposing east face of Pinnacle Buttress. It is almost certainly the best introduction to climbing in Coire Ardair, as it passes through some magnificent rock scenery.

The face of Pinnacle Buttress, which is sustained at a high angle, reaches a total height of nearly 1500 ft. The most outstanding climb of several on this face is undoubtedly *Smith's Gully* (600 ft.; Grade V), the central of three prominent slits on the upper left side of the face. It was first climbed by J. R. Marshall and G. Tiso in 1959 and

must rank as one of the most difficult winter climbs, certainly in Coire Ardair. *Easy Gully* (1500 ft.; Grade I) slants up leftwards to the plateau behind Pinnacle Buttress and under the Post Face, and as its name implies is the easiest route in the corrie. It passes through some impressive scenery and provides a convenient route of descent, although one should be particularly aware of the danger of avalanches from the Post Face, especially in thaw conditions.

The gullies, or Posts, which sever the Post Face and give it its name are the most prominent features of the corrie. There are four Posts. That on the left, the *Last Post* (800 ft.; Grade IV), was the last to fall, to T. W. Patey and R. F. Brooke in 1962. Both the *South Post* (1500 ft.; Grade III) and the *Centre Post* (1500 ft.; Grade III) – climbed respectively by N. S. Tennent and M. Slesser in 1956, and by C. M. Allan and J. H. B. Bell in 1937 – now have direct routes which must certainly rank with the hardest ice climbs in the country, while the ordinary routes on either Post are perhaps the finest expeditions of their kind in the corrie. Mention should also be made of the gigantic ice pitch of the *Centre Post Direct*, often vertical for close on 200 ft. and first climbed in 1964 by B. W. Robertson, F. Harper and E. Cairns. Discounting these direct routes, the *North Post* (1500 ft.; Grade V) is the hardest of the four and offers an outstanding winter climb. The right extremity of the Post Face is characterised by the Shelf, which slants up rightwards to the prominent parallel slits of the North and South Pipes. The Shelf and the North Pipe are known as *Staghorn Gully* (1500 ft.; Grade III). First done by C. M. Allan, J. H. B. Bell, H. M. Kelly and H. Couper in 1934, this is now a deservedly popular climb. The *South Pipe* (Grade IV), by J. H. B. Bell and Miss V. Roy in 1935, provides an excellent alternative finish to the climb.

The Post Face now swings round into the Inner Coire, an extensive line of cliffs tapering towards the Window, the col at the right-hand extremity of the cliffs. Routes are generally shorter and less serious than most of the others in Coire Ardair, but no less interesting. Probably the most prominent features are the huge parallel icefalls on the upper part of the cliff some distance beyond Staghorn Gully. These two icefalls, *Diadem* to the right (700 ft.; Grade IV), which was climbed by T. W. Patey and J. Brown in 1964, and *The Wand* to the left (700 ft.; Grade V), climbed by Q. Crichton, G. N. Hunter,

30. *Opposite :* Creag Meaghaidh: the cliffs of Coire Ardair.

31. Creag Meaghaidh: Coire Ardair and the Window.

D. F. Lang and N. Quinn in 1969, are outstanding attractions in the Inner Coire. A good mountaineering route, *The Sash* (800 ft.; Grade III), first climbed by T. W. Patey, R. W. P. Barclay, M. Laverty and E. Attfield in 1963, approaches the parallel icefalls directly and avoids them on the left. The prominent gully, *Cinderalla* (700 ft.; Grade II), in the centre, is the easiest route on the face, while the last gully worthy of note is *Crescent Gully* (700 ft.; Grade III), which curves up the left side of the large vertical wall next to the Window. Longest of the Inner Coire routes, *The Pumpkin*

(1000 ft.; Grade V), was made in 1968 by R. McMillan, G. Peet and N. Quinn.

Finally mention must be made of the winter *Girdle Traverse* of the Coire Ardair cliffs, the longest expedition of its kind in Great Britain (*c.*8000 ft.). Following reconnaissances by various parties, the entire traverse was finally done solo in a remarkable 5-hour *tour de force* by T. W. Patey in March 1969. Although graded only III–IV, fine situations are abundant, with much of the climbing serious and exposed. For complete details see article and descriptive notes in S.M.C.J. Vol. XXIX. No. 161. May 1970.

The development of Coire Ardair as a major winter climbing area is inexplicably retarded, the majority of the climbs having appeared in the last decade. There is still potential for good, modern, hard winter climbs, particularly on the buttresses.

For further full details reference should be made to the Guide Book, *Coire Ardair, Creag Meaghaidh – Winter*, by A. McKeith.

The conspicuous pass of the Window (3200 ft.) was probably used by Prince Charlie during his crossing into Badenoch from the Lochiel country on August 28, 1746. It is easily approached from Aberardair Farm, making use of the path already referred to as a helpful route into Coire Ardair. From the notch a simple climb of 250 ft. up grassy slopes, or, by keeping to the right, a scramble up broken rocks and boulders, places one on the first summit of the ridge continuing eastwards, **Poite Coire Ardair** (3460 ft.). The top is the south-west end of the 3250-ft. contour and overlooks Loch Roy, while the second top (3441 ft.), ½ mile north-east along the ridge, gives very fine views back to the cliffs of Coire Ardair. Another mile brings one to **Sròn Garbh Choire** (3250 ft.), the small contour on the one-inch O.S. map about ½ mile south-east of the name.

Càrn Liath (3298 ft.), along with its three subsidiary tops, may be taken in easily as a continuation of the ridge just described, first over the broad gentle slopes of **Meall an t-Snaim** (3180 ft.), then north-eastwards beyond the main summit over **A'Bhuidheanach** (3177 ft.) and **Stob Choire Dhuibh** (3002 ft.). Alternatively, from the scattering of woods on Loch Laggan-side 1½ miles west of Loch Laggan Hotel, a pleasant walk may be had across the moor – often busy with deer – and on to the ridge, with visits thereafter to as many tops as one fancies. To return to Loch Laggan from Stob Choire Dhuibh, one should strike due south so as to avoid the steep descent into Coire Dhuibh and the detour round Meall Ghoirleig. Alternatively the ridge can be followed $\frac{3}{4}$ mile to Càrn Dubh (2955 ft.) and then due east down to the path leading from the Corrieyairack road down to Loch Laggan Hotel.

BIBLIOGRAPHY

Coire Ardair, Creag Meaghaidh – Winter, A. McKeith. (Tiso. 1967.)
Highways and Byways in the Central Highlands, Seton Gordon. (Macmillan. 1948.)

18

The Monadh Liath

(1) **Gairbeinn** (2929 ft.). 2½ miles east of the Corrieyairack Pass.
(2) **Meall na h-Aisre** (2825 ft.). 3½ miles north of Garva Bridge.
(3) **Càrn a' Chuilinn** (2677 ft.). 4¼ miles south-east of Fort Augustus.
(4) **Càrn Easgann Bana** (2554 ft.). 7 miles E.S.E. of Fort Augustus.
(5) *****Geal Chàrn** (3036 ft.). 4 miles north-west of Laggan Bridge.
(6) *****Càrn Dearg, North Top** (3093 ft.). 5½ miles W.N.W. of Newtonmore.
(7) **Càrn Dearg, South Top** (3025 ft.). ½ mile S. by E. of (6).
(8) *****Càrn Bàn** (3087 ft.). ½ mile N.N.W. of (6).
(9) **Snechdach Slinnean** (3011 ft.). ⅔ mile W.S.W. of (8).
(10) *****Càrn Ballach** (3020 ft.). 1½ miles north-east of (8).
(11) *****Càrn Sgùlain** (3015 ft.). 2¼ miles E.N.E. of (10).
(12) *****A'Chailleach** (3045 ft.). 1 mile south of (11) and 3¾ miles N.N.W. of Newtonmore.
(13) **Càrn na Làraiche Maoile** (2658 ft.). 11½ miles north-west of Newtonmore.
(14) **Càrn na Saobhaidhe** (2658 ft.). 12 miles N.W. by W. of Newtonmore.
(15) **Càrn an Fhreiceadain** (2879 ft.). 4½ miles N.N.W. of Kingussie.
(16) **Geal-Chàrn Mòr** (2702 ft.). 3¾ miles west of Aviemore.

The aptly-named Monadh Liath, or 'grey moors', are situated wholly in Inverness-shire and extend eastwards from the Corrieyairack Pass along the north side of the River Spey, the main massif forming the watershed between that river and the headwaters of the Tarff, Fechlin, Findhorn and Dulnain.

The highest part of the range lies between Geal Chàrn, 4 miles north-west of Laggan Bridge, and Càrn Sgùlain, 5½ miles north-west of Kingussie. Within this area there are 8 distinct tops rising above the 3000-ft. contour line. At the head of the Dulnain the range divides into two branches, the one continuing the E.N.E. trend of the main range between the Spey and the Dulnain, the other running north-east between the valleys of the Dulnain and the Findhorn. Northwards again is a rampart of high moorland separating upper Strath Dearn from Strath Errick.

Considering the extent of the range and the height attained by its central portion, the Monadh Liath are – apart from Creag Dubh, near Newtonmore – singularly devoid of interest to the climber. The

F

range is in fact a wide, undulating plateau, with peat and fringe-moss covering stony debris. On the north side peat-covered slopes descend in dreary monotony to the headwaters of the Fechlin and Findhorn, and the rock features are confined almost entirely to the corries and glens that fall southwards into Strathspey. Some fair rock-scrambling is discoverable, notably in the corries round Lochan a' Choire and Loch Dubh, but otherwise the chief virtue of the group – again apart from Creag Dubh – lies in the fine high-level moorland walks to be enjoyed, with a wealth of far views, in particular of the Cairngorms. In winter and early spring, when snow conditions are right, it can be ideal country for the skier, with an atmosphere of spaciousness rarely excelled.

Forming the south-western edge of the Monadh Liath, the Pass of Corrieyairack (2543 ft.) was for centuries an important line of communication between the Western Highlands and the South. It was one of the old drove roads and, in the icy weather of January 1645, it played its part in that famous march of Montrose and his army which, according to John Buchan, 'is one of the great exploits in the history of British arms'. Seemingly trapped at Kilcumin – the Fort Augustus of today – with the Earl of Seaforth at Inverness in command of 5000 men, and 3000 Campbells, lusting for revenge, at Inverlochy, Montrose and his 1500 weary men moved unobtrusively south. Up the Tarff, over the pass to Glen Turret and down Glen Roy to the Spean the little force marched, all day, all night and into the next day, hungry and cold. Then, skirting the northern flanks of the Aonachs and Càrn Mòr Dearg, they launched their attack on Inverlochy, to shatter the might of Clan Campbell with terrible slaughter.

Exactly a hundred years later, in August 1745, Bonnie Prince Charlie used the Corrieyairack to reach Dalwhinnie from Invergarry. The Prince had hoped to bring General Cope's army to a decisive engagement in this favourable mountain terrain, but the English commander took discreet avoiding action by turning aside to Ruthven barracks near Kingussie, then moving north to Inverness through the defile of Slochd. The way to the Lowlands was now open to the Jacobites and they marched on south to Perth by way of Blair Atholl and Dunkeld.

It was fourteen years before this, in 1731, that General Wade completed his military road over the Pass leading from Dalwhinnie and Laggan Bridge up the headwaters of the Spey to Melgarve and then northwards over the summit and down the Allt Coire Uchdachan and Glen Tarff to Fort Augustus. In an old *Imperial Gazetteer of Scotland* there is a quotation from a traveller called Skrine who crossed the Pass by the road from north to south – in a carriage. He refers to the 'inexpressibly arduous road . . . elevated to a height truly terrific – springing sometimes from point to point over alpine bridges and at other times pursuing narrow ridges of rock frightfully impending over tremendous precipices'. Evidently a perfect paradise for rock-climbers! As a matter of fact, although the approaches on both sides are attractive, the upper parts of the route are rather tame and uninteresting, being among scenery typical of the Monadh Liath.

The road as constructed by General Wade left the Great North Road at Dalwhinnie and crossed over to the Spey valley near Laggan. The original intention was that it should branch off on the north side of the Spey at Laggan Bridge, curving round for 2 miles to recross the river by a large stone bridge. The latter was, in fact, never completed and is now in ruins. There is, however, a footbridge at this point, to which the more obvious direct route is from the main road $\frac{3}{4}$ mile west of Drumgask. The road then continues up the right bank of the Spey for 5 miles to Garva Bridge, where it crosses to the left, north bank. It is possible to take a car some 4 miles farther, to Melgarve, whence a subsidiary path runs west past Loch Spey, the source of the river, and over the col beyond (1151 ft.) into Glen Roy. Continuing to the summit of the pass, the last 500 ft. is steep and the rocky, grass-grown track ascends by 12 zigzags. At the cairn (2507 ft.) the route does not go down north into Coire na Cèire, but continues on west to 2543 ft., then descends by the Allt Coire Uchdachan to the Allt Lagan a' Bhainne. The important bridge over the latter, which had completely collapsed, was renewed in 1932 by the Scottish Rights of Way Society. Here, beside screening birches and near the knoll known as Prince Charlie's Breakfasting Hill, is pleasant camping ground. At Blackburn, $1\frac{1}{2}$ miles farther on, only rickles of stones remain of what was once no doubt a thriving little roadside clachan.

The start of the track at the northern end is $\frac{1}{4}$ mile along the side road which leaves the main A82 opposite Loch Uanagan $1\frac{1}{2}$ miles south of Fort Augustus. A battered notice erected by the Scottish Rights of Way Society announces 'Wade's Road to Laggan'. After some 200 yards the track assumes the properties of a stream-bed and thereafter is best left to Land-Rovers.

Gairbeinn (2929 ft.) is easily reached from the Corrieyairack track ½ mile beyond Melgarve by way of its south-western slopes, **Meall na h-Aisre** (2825 ft.) probably rather more wearily after a 3½-mile trudge northwards from Garva Bridge. **Càrn a' Chuilinn** (2677 ft.), overlooking a chain of lochans in the heart of the Glendoe Forest, may be climbed from Glen Tarff, while **Càrn Easgann Bana** (2554 ft.) is considerably more remote, a moorland eminence east of the head of Glen Brein.

Geal Chàrn (3036 ft.) is a bulky mountain on the west side of Glen Markie, with a deep, east-facing corrie enclosing Lochan a' Choire. Cutting through the rocks at the head of this corrie is one of the numerous 'windows' of the district, Uinneag a' Choire Lochain. A good path up Glen Markie from Crathie is initially of some help; higher, a slight dip separates Beinn na Sgiath (2845 ft.), the broad and mossy south top, from the well-cairned main summit.

From Glen Markie an old drove road, marked by cairns, leads across the Monadh Liath to Loch Ness-side. The route starts at Laggan Bridge, goes west to Crathie, then turns north and north-west, to cross the watershed to Loch na Lairige, dropping beyond by the east side of the Allt Crom to Sronlairig Lodge. From here a road leads down past Loch Killin and beside the River Fechlin to the Fort Augustus road ½ mile west of Whitebridge Inn. Total distance about 22 miles.

Càrn Dearg, North Top (3093 ft.) and **South Top** (3025 ft.). This mountain forms a narrow spur projecting S.S.E. from the main plateau and falling abruptly on the east into Gleann Ballach, on the west into the picturesque Coire Lochain. The summit is finely placed above the steep eastern crags. It is best ascended from New-tonmore up the Calder into Glen Banchor and thence by the path on the east side of the Allt Fionndrigh for about 2 miles. The way then leads across the burn and west over the broad, peaty saddle north of Creag Liath, whence one can contour round the head of Glen Ballach to the ridge between Càrn Dearg and Càrn Bàn. The south top lies ½ mile from the northern.

32. Monadh Liath: near the head of Glen Banchor.

Càrn Bàn (3087 ft.) is a rather tame summit, though the highest point of the main plateau. Formerly known as Càrn Mairg, it is only ½ mile from Càrn Dearg and separated by a dip of 160 ft. On its W.S.W. top, **Snechdach Slinnean** (3011 ft.), the Red Burn rises, flowing farther down through a remarkable rock gorge with water-falls, worthy of exploration, before it increases in importance to become the Markie Burn.

Càrn Ballach (3020 ft.) and **Càrn Sgùlain** (3015 ft.) are no more than rather featureless eminences above the general level of the summit plateau. **A'Chailleach** (3045 ft.), even more easily reached from Newtonmore by the Allt na Féithe Buidhe track, has the distinction of a fairly steep rock face on the east forming Coire na Cailleach and Bruthach nan Easain, the 'hillside of the water-falls'. All are, of course, especially suitable for ski-ing under good conditions, one worth-while run being south-eastwards from the summit of A'Chailleach down past the Red Hut to the Allt a' Chaoruinn.

For those who delight in hunting down remote and obscure 'Corbetts', the moorland eminences **Càrn na Làraiche Maoile** (2658 ft.) and **Càrn na Saobhaidhe** (2658 ft.) should be found particularly satisfying. The former lies 3½ miles east of Loch Killin, the latter another 2¼ miles N.N.W. in the still lonelier wilderness above the headwaters of the Findhorn. By contrast, **Càrn an Fhreiceadain** (2879 ft.) presents an easier problem, being reached by its southern slopes from the pleasant track up the Gynack behind Kingussie golf course. **Geal-Chàrn Mòr** (2702 ft.), 3¾ miles west of Aviemore, is also readily accessible, from the hill-track which leaves the A9 at Easter Lynwilg and crosses over to the Dulnain.

At a lower level, Craigellachie crag behind the Cairngorm Hotel in Aviemore has one named rock-route, the central slanting groove and face above – *Kretin*. 250 ft. Very severe. (D. Haston and T. Good-ing. October 1964.) Also of interest are the slabs below and to the left of the main face, while 350 ft. to the right there is a watercourse which can give a hard 200-ft. ice-climb.

Creag Dubh – Overlooking the main Newtonmore–Spean Bridge road just over 3 miles from Newtonmore, Creag Dubh presents to the rock-climber what has been described as 'the finest low-level crag in the country'. Easily reached within five or ten minutes from the road, the three cliffs concerned offer a variety of routes up to 450 ft. in length, mostly of very high standard. Facing south, they dry quickly after rain and in winter are frequently clear and warm when other, higher areas are under snow. The rock is mica-schist and sound for the most part, though requiring a wide selection of pegs as there are few natural belays. Flat holds on steep or overhanging walls, with a number of impressive roofs, characterise the climbing.

The true worth of Creag Dubh was not realised until 1959 when the first three routes were pioneered. These were followed by single discoveries in August 1962 and October 1964, then in 1965 by an avalanche of no less than 27 new routes and 5 variations. In the next four years a further 10 routes were added.

The area comprises three main cliffs: Bedtime Buttress on the left, a large rounded buttress characterised by a prominent roof on its upper right-hand side; Central Wall, including Waterfall Wall and The Great Wall, with some of the longest and finest of the routes; and Sprawl Wall, distinguished by a prominent, slanting fault.

For detailed descriptions of the routes themselves reference should be made to the rock-guide, 'Creag Dubh and the Eastern Outcrops', published by Graham Tiso, 44 Rodney Street, Edinburgh.

BIBLIOGRAPHY

Climbers' Guide to Creag Dubh and the Eastern Outcrops, G. Tiso. (Tiso. 1967.)

Highways and Byways in the Central Highlands, Seton Gordon. (Macmillan. 1948.)

The Marquis of Montrose, John Buchan. (Nelson. 1913.)

Transactions of the Inverness Scientific Society, Vol. V, pp. 145 and 364. (Two papers on the Corrieyairack and other military roads, by Sir Kenneth S. Mackenzie, Bt., of Gairloch.)

Mountain Names and Meanings

The following list attempts to give the meanings of the mountain names mentioned in the Guide. It is impossible to give satisfactory explanations for all names: some are doubtful, and these have been indicated by question-marks; others, left blank, are still wholly puzzling.

Grateful thanks are due to Dr. W. F. H. Nicolaisen, Acting Head of the School of Scottish Studies, Edinburgh University, and to his colleague on the Scottish Place-Name Survey, Mr. Ian A. Fraser, for checking the list and suggesting a number of most interesting interpretations. Gaelic spellings, as in the Guide itself, are those of Munro's Tables; where amended spellings have been suggested, these are added in brackets.

A'Bhuidheanach: *yellow ridge.*
A'Chailleach: *old wife.*
A'Mharconaich:
Am Bodach: *the old man.*
An Cearcallach: *the hoop.*
An Garbhanach: *the rough ridge.*
An Gearanach: *the short ridge.*
An t-Sròn: *the nose.*
Aonach Beag: *little ridge, or moor.*
Aonach Dubh: *black ridge.*
Aonach Eagach: *notched ridge.*
Aonach Mòr: *great ridge, or moor.*

Beinn a' Bheithir: *peak of the thunderbolt, or monster* (?).
Beinn a' Bhùiridh: *hill of roaring (stags).*
Beinn a' Chaoruinn: *mountain of the rowan tree.*
Beinn a' Chlachair: *mason's mountain.*
Beinn a' Chochuill: *mountain of the hood.*
Beinn a' Chrulaiste:

Beinn a' Chuallaich: *mountain of herding.*
Beinn Bheòil: *mountain in front (of Ben Alder).*
Beinn Ceitlein:
Beinn Chumhainn: *narrow mountain.*
Beinn Eibhinn: *mountain with a fair outlook.*
Beinn Eunaich: *fowling peak.*
Beinn Fhada: *long mountain.*
Beinn Fhionnlaidh: *Finlay's mountain.*
Beinn Iaruinn: *iron mountain.*
Beinn Maol Chaluim: *Calum's bare mountain.*
Beinn Mhic Chasgaig:
Beinn Mhic-Mhonaidh: *mountain of the son of the moor* (?).
Beinn Mholach: *shaggy mountain.*
Beinn na Lap: *boggy mountain* (?).
Beinn nan Aighean: *mountain of the hinds.*
Beinn Sgulaird:
Beinn Teallach:
Beinn Trilleachan: *mountain of sandpipers.*
Beinn Udlamain: *mountain of the unsteady place.*
Ben Alder: *mountain of rock and water.*
Ben Cruachan: *mountain of peaks, or stacks.*
Ben Nevis: *venomous, malicious mountain.*
Ben Starav: *strong, or stout mountain.*
Bidean nam Bian: *pinnacle of the hides.*
Binnein Beag: *little hill.*
Binnein Mòr: *big hill.*
Buachaille Etive Beag: *the little herdsman of Etive.*
Buachaille Etive Mòr: *the great herdsman of Etive.*

Caisteal: *the castle.*
Càrn a' Chuilinn: *cairn of the holly.*
Càrn an Fhreiceadain: *cairn of the watcher.*
Càrn B(e)allach: *cairn of the pass.*
Càrn Bàn: *white cairn.*
Càrn Beag Dearg: *little red cairn.*
Càrn Dearg: *red cairn.*
Càrn Dearg Meadhonach: *middle red cairn.*
Càrn Easgann Bana: *cairn of the white eels* (?).
Càrn Liath: *grey cairn.*
Càrn Mòr Dearg: *big red cairn.*

Càrn na Laraiche Maoile: *cairn of the bare site, or ruin.*
Càrn na Saobhaidhe: *cairn of the fox's den.*
Càrn Sgùlain: *cairn of the basket.*
Chno Dearg: *red nut.*
Clach Leathad: *stony slope.*
Creach Bheinn: *mountain of prey or spoil.*
Creag Dubh: *black rock.*
Creag Meaghaidh:
Creag Mhòr: *great rock.*
Creag Pitridh: *rock of the hollow places.*
Crèise:
Cruach Innse: *stack of the meadow.*

Diollaid a' Chàirn: *saddle of the cairn.*
Drochaid Glas: *grey bridge.*

Fara, The (G. faradh): *ladder.*
Fraochaidh: *place of heather.*

Gairbeinn: *rough mountain.*
Garbh Bheinn: *rough mountain.*
Geal-Chàrn: *white cairn.*
Geal-Chàrn Mòr: *big white cairn.*
Geàrr Aonach: *short height, or ridge.*
Glas Bheinn: *grey mountain.*
Glas Bheinn Mhòr: *big grey mountain.*

Leum Uilleim: *William's leap.*

Mam Coire Easain: *moor, or plateau of the corrie of the waterfalls.*
Mam na Gualainn: *plateau of the shoulder.*
Meall a' Bhùiridh: *hill of the roaring (stags).*
Meall an t-Snaim: *hill of the knot.*
Meall Cruidh: *hill of the shoe.*
Meall Cuanail: *seaward-looking hill (?).*
Meall Dearg: *red hill.*
Meall Garbh: *rough hill.*
Meall na h-Aisre: *hill of the defile.*
Meall na Leitreach: *hill of slopes.*
Meall nan Eun: *hill of the birds.*

Mullach Coire an Iubhair: *top of the corrie of the yew tree.*
Mullach Coire Choille-rais: *top of the corrie of the shrub wood.*
Mullach Coire nan Nead: *top of the corrie of the nests.*
Mullach nan Coirean: *top of the corries.*

Na Gruagaichean: *the maidens.*

Poite (Poit) Coire Ardair: *pot of the high corrie.*
Puist Coire Ardair: *post of the high corrie.*

Sgairneach Mhòr: *big rocky hillside.*
Sgòr Chòinnich: *Kenneth's peak.*
Sgòr Gaibhre: *peak of the goats.*
Sgòr Iutharn: *hell's peak* (?).
Sgòr na h-Ulaidh: *peak of the hidden treasure.*
Sgòr nam Fiannaidh: *peak of the Fianns.*
Sgòr an Iubhair: *peak of the yew tree.*
Sgòrr Bhan: *white peak.*
Sgòrr Dhearg: *red peak.*
Sgòrr Dhonuill: *Donald's peak.*
Sgùrr a' Bhuic: *peak of the buck.*
Sgùrr a' Mhaim: *peak of the pass.*
Sgùrr Chòinnich Beag: *little mossy peak.*
Sgùrr Chòinnich Mòr: *big mossy peak.*
Sgùrr Eilde Beag: *little crag of the hinds.*
Sgùrr Eilde Mòr: *big crag of the hinds.*
Sgùrr Innse: *peak of the meadow.*
Sne(a)chdach Slinnean: *snowy shoulder-blade.*
Sròn a' Ghearrain: *nose of the gelding.*
Sròn an Isean: *nose of the young bird, or chick.*
Sròn Coire na h-Iolaire: *nose of the eagles' corrie.*
Sròn Garbh: *rough nose.*
Sròn Garbh Choire: *nose of the rough corrie.*
Sròn nan Giubhas: *nose of the firs.*
Stob a' Bhruaich Lèith: *peak of the grey brae.*
Stob a' Choire Lèith: *peak of the grey corrie.*
Stob a' Choire Mheadhoin: *peak of the middle corrie.*
Stob a' Choire Odhair: *peak of the dun corrie.*
Stob a' Ghlais Choire: *peak of the grey corrie.*
Stob an Aonaich Mhòir: *peak of the big ridge, or moor.*

Stob an Cul Choire: *peak at the back of the corrie.*
Stob an Fhuarain: *peak of the well.*
Stob Bàn: *white peak.*
Stob Choire Claurigh:
Stob Choire Dhuibh: *peak of the black corrie.*
Stob Coir' an Albannaich: *peak of the corrie of the Scotsman.*
Stob Coire Altruim: *peak of the nursing corrie (hinds with calves).*
Stob Coire a' Chairn: *peak of the stony corrie.*
Stob Coire an Easain: *peak of the corrie of the waterfalls.*
Stob Coire an Fhir Dhuibh: *peak of the corrie of the black man.*
Stob Coire an Laoigh: *peak of the corrie of the calf.*
Stob Coire Bhealaich: *peak of the corrie of the pass.*
Stob Coire Cath na Sine: *peak of the corrie of the battle of storm (?).*
Stob Coire Dheirg: *peak of the red corrie.*
Stob Coire Gaibhre: *peak of the corrie of the goats.*
Stob Coire Lèith: *peak of the grey corrie.*
Stob Coire nam Beith: *peak of the corrie of the birch trees.*
Stob Coire na Ceannain: *peak of the corrie of the bluff.*
Stob Coire nan Lochan: *peak of the corrie of the lochans.*
Stob Coire Raineach: *peak of the corrie of the ferns.*
Stob Coire Sgreamhach: *peak of the rocky corrie.*
Stob Coire Sgriodain: *peak of the scree corrie.*
Stob Dearg: *red peak.*
Stob Diamh (Daimh): *peak of the stags.*
Stob Dubh: *black peak.*
Stob Garbh: *rough peak.*
Stob Ghabhar: *peak of the goats.*
Stob na Bròige: *peak of the shoe.*
Stob na Doire: *peak of the copse.*

Tom na Sròine: *hill of the nose.*

Uinneag a' Ghlas Choire: *window of the grey corrie.*

Advice to Hill-Walkers

The Scottish Climbing Clubs consider it desirable to give advice to hill-walkers – especially to those with limited knowledge of conditions in Scotland. The present time is appropriate as an increasing number of people make use of the Scottish mountains in summer and in winter.

The Clubs are constrained to give this advice owing to the accidents in recent years which led to serious injury or death, caused trouble and anxiety to local residents called from their ordinary vocations, and to experienced climbers summoned from long distances to render assistance. Such assistance must not be regarded as always available, and it is only fair and reasonable that local helpers be paid adequately for their assistance.

The guide books issued by the Scottish Mountaineering Club describe routes which range from difficult climbs to what are in fine weather mere walks. It cannot be stressed too strongly that an expedition, which in fine weather is simple, may cease to be so if the weather becomes bad or mist descends. In winter, conditions on the hills change – what in summer is a walk may become a mountaineering expedition.

In many cases accidents are caused by a combination of events, no one of which singly would have been serious. Ample time should be allowed for expeditions, especially when the route is unknown. Further, before setting out on an expedition, parties should leave information as to their objectives and route and, without exception, have the courage to turn back when prudence so dictates.

In expeditions of any magnitude a party should consist of not less than three members, and they should never separate. If the party is large, two of the experienced members should bring up the rear.

If one member of the party is injured, another member should stay with him with all available food and spare clothing, while the remainder go to secure help. Great care should be taken in marking the spot where the injured man is left. Unless a conspicuous landmark is chosen, for example the junction of two streams, it is difficult to locate the spot, especially if the return is from a different direction or by night.

Some common causes of difficulty are:
Underestimate of time required for expedition.
Slow or untried companions or members who are in poor training.
Illness caused through unwise eating or drinking.
Extreme cold or exhaustion through severe conditions.
Poor, soft snow; steep hard snow; snowstorms; mist.
Change in temperature rapidly converting soft snow into ice – involving step cutting.
Rain making rock slippery or snow filling the holds when rock climbing.
Frost after snow or rain glazing rocks with ice.
Sudden spates rendering the crossing of burns dangerous or impossible and necessitating long detours.

Hints – Equipment:
All parties should carry:

Simple First Aid equipment, torch, whistle, watch, one-inch Ordnance Survey map, compass, and be able to use them.

Except in a few spots in Skye where the rocks are magnetic, the compass direction is certain to be correct even if it differs from one's sense of direction.

Ice axes should be carried if there is any chance of snow or ice, and a rope unless it is certain not to be required.

Clothing: At all times reserve clothing should be carried. Temperatures change rapidly, especially at high levels. Clothing should be warm; in winter a Balaclava helmet and thick woollen gloves should be carried. Well-shod boots should always be worn.

Food: Each member of a party should carry his own food. Climbers will find from experience what kind of food suits their individual need. Normally, jams and sugar are better than meat as more rapidly converted into energy. Most people will find it advisable to avoid alcohol on the hills, but a flask may be carried for emergencies. Light meals at frequent intervals are better than heavy meals at long intervals. In winter it may be advisable to make an early stop for food if shelter is found.

It is essential at all times to respect proprietary and sporting rights, especially during the shooting season, and to avoid disturbing game in deer forests and on grouse moors.

Issued with the authority of

Scottish Mountaineering Club
Dundee Rambling Club
Ladies' Scottish Climbing Club
Moray Mountaineering Club
Creagh Dhu Mountaineering Club
Edinburgh University Mountaineering Club
Cairngorm Club
Grampian Club
Lomond Mountaineering Club
Junior Mountaineering Club of Scotland
Etchachan Club

INDEX

NOTE TO READER

The District Guide Book Series issued by the Scottish Mountaineering Trust has been published since the early 1920s. A list of titles appears at the front of this book. Earlier editions included rock climbs and serious mountaineering routes in summer and winter conditions. The series is now being progressively re-written to satisfy the increasing demand for regional information and particular outdoor pursuits on mountains. For the first time illustrations have been integrated with the text of each book and a map in five colours is bound into the volumes as an endpaper.

Established rock climbing areas within the regions described in the District Guide Book Series are being removed for separate publication in a pocket-size series of guide books, also of new format and design.

Published simultaneously with this new style District guide for *The Central Highlands* is THE CAIRNGORMS by Sir Henry Alexander. THE NORTHERN HIGHLANDS by Thomas Strang is due to appear in May, 1969. Also during 1969, MUNRO'S TABLES will be re-issued.

Among the new series rock climbing guide books to appear during 1969 are:

CUILLIN OF SKYE in two volumes
NORTHERN HIGHLANDS in three volumes
BEN NEVIS
ARROCHAR

A complete catalogue of all Scottish Mountaineering Trust publications is now available, and members of the public can obtain copies by remitting 7d in stamps to the producers, to whom all public and trade inquiries should be addressed:

West Col Productions, 1 Meadow Close, Goring, Reading RG8 OAP, Berkshire, England.

December, 1968